HONOLULU CSI

AN INTRODUCTION TO FORENSIC SCIENCE AND CRIMINAL INVESTIGATION

Gary A. Dias and Robbie Dingeman

Illustrations by Joe Aragon and Chun Yee

3565 Harding Ave.
Honolulu, Hawai'i 96816
Phone: (800) 910-2377
Fax: (808) 732-3627
www.besspress.com

Design: Carol Colbath

Dias, Gary A.
  Honolulu CSI : an introduction to
forensic science and criminal
investigation / Gary A. Dias and
Robbie Dingeman.
        p.   cm.
  Includes illustrations.
  ISBN 1-57306-228-6
  1. Crime scene searches - Hawaii -
Honolulu. 2. Criminal investigation -
Hawaii - Honolulu. 3. Evidence, Criminal -
Hawaii - Honolulu. 4. Crime - Hawaii -
Honolulu. 5. Crime prevention.
I. Dingeman, Robbie. II. Title.
HV8073.D52 2004   363.2-dc21

Printed in Korea

For
Ryan, Kevin, Samantha, Alexis,
and the rest of our families

And for all the investigators and
crime scene technicians
who care about doing it right the first time

Contents

OXYGEN

FUEL   HEAT

Bonus Section: Protect Yourself in a Dangerous World

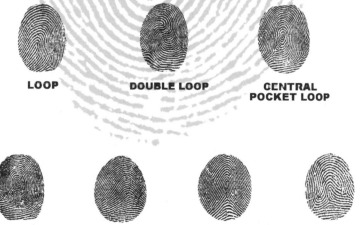

LOOP   DOUBLE LOOP   CENTRAL
POCKET LOOP

PLAIN WHORL   PLAIN ARCH   TENTED ARCH   ACCIDENTAL

Preface

In the years I spent as a police officer, particularly the years I spent as the lieutenant-in-charge of the Homicide Detail, my detectives and I became more and more dependent upon forensic science as a tool for obtaining evidence we could use to identify and convict murderers. Robbie was at the scene of many of those murders as a reporter. After our marriage, she often commented that the use of forensic techniques was frequently the leading cause of our success.

In what seemed to be a few short years, forensic science exploded into a vast field of procedures and techniques available to law enforcement, if only we would take the time to look and see what was available and accept these new tools. We did that in Honolulu, and in a matter of just a few years we caught up with mainland departments. Credit for this must go to people who had the foresight to believe that change and advancement in CSI actually was a good thing.

We must recognize people such as Retired Chief Michael Nakamura, Retired Assistant Chief Robert Kane, Retired Major Wilson Sullivan, and the men of the Homicide Detail: Rufus Kaukani, Andy Glushenko, Vernon "Bully" Santos, Earl Hirai, John Isabelo, Paul Putzulu (now a deputy chief of police—go Paul), Anderson Hee, James Kinimaka, Cliff Rubio, Steve Dung, Kenneth Ikehara (whose name was inadvertently left out of *Honolulu Cop*—sorry, Ken), and all the crime scene technicians and lab technicians who taught us what CSI is all about.

I would also like to acknowledge the two talented men of the Honolulu Police Department's Graphic Artist Unit, Joe Aragon and Chun Yee. Working with Joe and Chun, who developed the line drawings used in this book, has always been a pleasure, whether we were working on a homicide or a community event.

During the six years I was assigned to the Homicide Detail, the excellent work of the Graphic Artist Unit came through again and again. Later, when I was assigned to the Scientific Investigation Section, I got a close-up look at the magic worked by these two professionals.

Perhaps the most interesting work, yet not the most urgent, was the reconstruction of the bust of Detective Chang Apana, the Honolulu detective who was the basis for Earl Derr Biggers' legendary Honolulu detective Charlie Chan. The bust was done from old 1920s photos we had in our police library. Apana's bust was used as a part of the Sherlock Holmes Night adventures that I wrote and developed for HPD between 1992 and 1998.

Introduction

When *Honolulu Homicide* was published, Robbie and I were approached by many people who asked—and in some cases the more aggressive ones demanded—that she and I do a third book on the subject of crime scene investigation (CSI). A great number of them told us, "I read your book, and I really liked the way you described how the police investigated the crime scene. Just like that TV show— what were those letters?"

While *Honolulu Homicide* does tell a little about the "what" that goes on behind the scenes at a criminal investigation, we focus primarily on the cases and not the forensic techniques—the "how" or sometimes the "why" involved with CSI. For this book, we have again chosen the crime of homicide to represent the offense in which the forensic technique is applied. If the technique works for the murder case, it will work for all others.

In any enterprise, we will succeed when our foundations are properly set. There are five major foundational considerations that one should understand when taking on the task of investigating the crime scene of a murder. First, there is the concept of *organization*. Whatever we do in life, we normally do in an organized manner. The last thing you need to hear from a detective at a murder scene is, "Gee, what do we do now?" Organization will help the detective move forward through an investigation more confidently and will help assure that the rest of the foundation is strong.

Second, we must be *thorough* in what we do. Thoroughness is an absolute must for any investigation. We don't (or *shouldn't*) go through life with the attitude that we're going to make a half-assed effort. Think about this scenario: You're going into the operating room for heart surgery and you overhear the surgeon telling one of the nurses, "Nice day today, huh? My golf game is at noon, and I gotta stop by the pro shop for a few balls. Let's get this done quick. I know a few shortcuts that will shave an hour off this procedure." That would make you want to get up and run. Unfortunately, the dead guy at the murder scene can't do that. At major crime scenes, detectives normally have only one chance to process that scene as thoroughly as possible. When they leave the scene and open it up to the public, they open it to terminal contamination. Untold numbers of curious people will walk through it, touch things, and ruin detectives' ability to say in court that they gathered evidence that was pure and uncontaminated.

Third, whatever we do, we must do with *caution*. Knowledge of what must be done at crime scenes is important in order to prevent damaging evidence through the use of a particular procedure. What goes first? What cannot wait? How do we get this knowledge? It is gained through experience, training, and education. The police agency simply cannot expect to develop expert detectives through on-the-job training.

Fourth comes the concept of *kīnā'ole*. We discussed this concept throughout *Honolulu Homicide*. It's a belief that came through the ages from the Hawaiians of old, and it deals with the attitude we carry through life on how we do things—how we perform our tasks and duties. *Kīnā'ole* means *doing the right thing, in the right way, at the right time, in the right place, to the right person, for the right reason, with the right feeling—the first time.*

We must credit the late George Kanahele, who taught this concept to the family of employees at The Queen's Medical Center. It is a belief that is simply put, yet deeply important to investigators—particularly homicide investigators who must always remember that, no matter the age of the deceased person, someone's child was murdered.

Finally, an *understanding of the laws* that govern what we may and may not do at crime scenes is essential. This understanding must be coupled with a belief in the system that we live by—the Bill of Rights that our forefathers fought and died for. We cannot ignore the "rules." People sometimes say that cops must abide by all the rules and the crooks have none. That's a true statement. And our integrity keeps us from violating those rules, because if we do, we run the risk of losing a conviction in court and setting the criminal or killer free.

One major law that forms the basic foundation of criminal investigation in the United States is the Fourth Amendment to the Constitution, which reads as follows:

The right of the people to be secure in their persons, houses, papers, and effects, against unreasonable searches and seizures, shall not be violated, and no warrants shall issue, but upon probable cause, supported by oath or affirmation, and particularly describing the place to be searched, and the persons or things to be seized.

Several concepts described in the Fourth Amendment are important to investigators. One is *unreasonableness.* The amendment does not prohibit searches and seizures—only those that are unreasonable. *Probable cause* is an abstract concept that is usually defined as "that condition or state that exists whereby a reasonable person would believe that a person committed a crime or was about to commit a crime." Who's reasonable? Not the cops. Not the prosecutors. The general public is considered reasonable. They have no personal criminal justice stake in the issue at hand. Finally, there is *particularity*. Detectives can't go to a place and search and recover items just because they want to or because they have an unfounded suspicion. They must be able to describe the place and the items they're looking for based on probable cause.

Too often, detectives rush through an investigation without a search warrant on the excuse that it's too time consuming. But it's really not. Some may think, "Hey, it's a crime scene—I can do what I like." But if it's a crime scene, it should be under the investigator's control, and it can be sealed off. There are times when certain crime scenes fall into a gray area of law and precedent. This could result in the loss of evidence—or even the case. The warrant will help protect the investigator's efforts.

"But the bosses don't want to spend overtime money!" Well, now, isn't that a kick in the pants? Administrators will tell detectives, "Go do the best job you can, but do it between the hours of 8 A.M. and 4:30 P.M., and be mindful of not spending too much overtime; you know that the city's budget is lacking again this year."

In *Honolulu Homicide,* we write about the Roland Kotani murder. Kotani, a state representative, was found bludgeoned to death in the master bedroom of his home. We were told by the administration that money for the investigation was no object—find his killer in a few days. We later joked that we worked too fast and didn't get enough of that "money is no object" rule. I couldn't help but wonder if we would get the same response for an unknown homeless person murdered in an alleyway off Hotel Street.

Organization, thoroughness, caution, *kīnā'ole,* and a strong belief in the foundations of law are critical ingredients in the trek toward successful investigations. Indeed, CSIs and forensic techniques can be akin to a journey. We move through the crime scene searching for evidence, looking for those items that can tie the suspect to the victim or vice versa. We traverse the different categories of evidence—fingerprints, trace evidence, and serology, to name a few—and the knowledge of different techniques and procedures.

It can be one of the most interesting trips anyone could ever take.

1
Crime Scenes

I once heard a detective grumble that he was fed up with the inconsistencies he saw at crime scenes. I asked him what he meant, and he told me that every time he was called to a crime scene, the officers protected the scene differently. Some scenes were big and broad, some too small. Some scenes had people walking all over them, and some had emergency medical technicians (EMTs) complaining that they were not allowed to do their job the right way.

I thought to myself that he was just a grumpy old man (no reference to the movie). At the time, I didn't realize that in his grumbling he was unwittingly describing what should (or shouldn't) be happening at crime scenes. In reality, the crime scene should reflect the needs of the investigation. In addition to his complaint of inconsistency, he was suggesting that the beat officers were not properly protecting the crime scenes in the first place. It seems to me now, looking back, that this was what he really wanted to say.

Years later when I took over the Homicide Detail, Captain Wilson Sullivan of the Scientific Investigation Section and I realized that many beat officers needed training on the aspects of a crime scene. So for the next few years we took on that task.

So What Is a Crime Scene?

Many people will say, confidently, that a crime scene is where the crime occurred. If you were answering this question on one of my college exams, you would be wrong. You would be wrong because that answer is not complete. A crime scene is indeed that physical location where the crime was committed. But it includes any location where evidence of the crime was located, and it includes the avenues of the suspect's approach to and escape from the crime scene.

Too often, law enforcement officers forget that the location of a bloody knife, even if it's found three hundred yards from a stabbing, should be considered a crime scene. And it should be protected as a crime scene, and it should be processed as a crime scene. Also, the possible approaches to and escapes from a crime scene should be examined very carefully for any evidence left by the suspect. Evidence such as footprints, tire prints, or any object dropped by the suspect could become critical evidence in the investigation.

In 'Ewa Beach a young man with a personality disorder shot his mother to death and buried her body under some ground cover in his backyard. Neighbors called police just before the killing because he was outside playing with his rifle. When officers arrived, they found the body but not the rifle.

Watch the approach to that scene

When we checked further we found that under one of the police vehicles parked in the driveway of the home was a rifle bullet. This was important because neighbors reported that the woman's son was loading and ejecting rounds on the driveway just before the shooting occurred. Since we did not immediately find the weapon, we realized that we might be able to tie the round on the driveway to the bullet recovered from the dead woman's body. Therefore, the officer could not leave until we finished processing that area; he had to wait for over an hour. We eventually found the rifle hidden in the attic, and the son was charged with murder.

Crime Scene Preservation

What is crime scene preservation? This is another trick question for my students. Invariably, they say, "Protecting the crime scene." That's not good enough. I hide my inner feelings of glee as I look upon their frustrated faces. "What more could it possibly be?" they ask. Like the definition of a crime scene, however, this answer has more than one segment. As defined by many criminalists and law enforcement scholars, *crime scene preservation is keeping the crime scene in the same condition as it was left by the perpetrator and preventing adding to or removing from the crime scene any items that may be evidence.*

This is done in many different ways. The most common visual effect you see of crime scene preservation is the use of crime scene barrier tape. The yellow plastic tape that officers stretch across crime scenes is usually the most convenient means of protecting the areas. Lacking this tape, however, police officers themselves become the barriers to prevent the public from entering crime scenes and tampering with evidence.

We would tell officers to extend the barrier tape or other security barriers well beyond the crime scenes. There are many reasons for this. After the Troy Barboza murder in 1987 (described in *Honolulu Homicide*), we made the error of running the crime scene barrier tape parallel with the street. That meant that anyone, including the media, could come right up to the very edge of the crime scene. In our frustration and shock at responding to the murder of a fellow officer, we failed to take into account that the suspect may have left evidence on the roadway that we left open to the public. We should have blocked the roadway at least a hundred yards in either direction until it could be examined for any possible evidence.

By extending the boundaries of a crime scene, we automatically protect that scene for a distance that could yield additional evidence that the suspect may have dropped in his approach or flight. While any item of evidence found outside the crime scene boundaries can be recovered and used in court, evidence protected by crime scene barriers that keep the public and media out tends to show the court and jury a greater degree of noncontamination of that item.

By keeping the crime scene in the condition we find it, we hope-fully ensure that investigators are able to view the scene as it was when the perpetrator left. From this perspective, we can perhaps gain a lead in reconstruction and identify those items touched or removed by the perpetrator. (Robbie, incidentally, does not like the word "perpetrator," believing that it is awkward police jargon. That's the journalist in her. The word does, however, specifically refer to the person responsible for committing the offense.)

The prevention of adding or removing things from the crime scene that may be evidence may seem a bit unnecessary since the police are protecting the scene—or are they? Aside from deliberately touching and removing items of evidence, as we saw done by the patrol captain in the murder of State Representative Roland Kotani, discussed in *Honolulu Homicide,* inquisitive police officers add and remove items from crime scenes all the time.

This happens simply by walking into a crime scene. The bottoms of our shoes or slippers are havens for tiny fragments of glass, strands of hair, lengths of fiber, pieces of rock and soil, and myriad other things that can be carried into and deposited in a crime scene. Just as frustrating is the fact that when officers or other people walk around the crime scene, they pick up those same items on the soles of their shoes or slippers and take them out of the crime scene when they leave. Those lost items could have been critical evidence linking a suspect to the victim or scene. It's up to that first officer or group of officers to ensure that the scene is properly preserved and protected from contamination.

Let's divert our attention for a minute and answer a question: "What makes a good police officer?" There could be several pages of answers, but one characteristic I would like to see in a police officer is *inquisitiveness.*

But inquisitiveness can also be a flaw when it comes to crime scene preservation. In the Roland Kotani murder investigation, we found some fingerprints near Kotani's body that didn't belong to his killer (later discovered to be his wife). Our investigation showed that those prints actually belonged to one of the initial police officers assigned to the crime scene. This officer, with great tenacity, insisted that he did not touch anything. In discussing the officer's actions at the scene, we learned that he checked the pulse of the deceased to determine if the victim was dead or not. It then dawned on us that in doing so, the officer probably lost his balance and reached out to steady himself, a natural reaction that is easily forgotten. You can prove this yourself at the end of this chapter.

Safe Pathway

It must be remembered that the word "contamination" is a descriptive one, not necessarily a bad one. Contamination will occur at crime scenes mostly out of need: the need to treat injured people, the need to ensure that the scene is safe, and so on. It therefore becomes imperative to control the response to the need. To do this, a *safe pathway* must be identified. But even before that, the first officers must ensure the scene is safe from culprits who might be hiding there.

It makes no sense for an officer to be hurt or killed while responding to a crime scene. How can the police help victims when they become victims themselves? It may seem cruel that the police don't rush in to immediately assist victims, but the reality is that they must first protect the victims *and* themselves from further injury.

When the scene is clear—that is, free from further danger—the officers can turn their attention to victims. At this point, the officers need to use their good judgment and determine a safe pathway through the scene to the victims. They must:

1. Find a trail or lane that looks the least disturbed. Normally that is the location of the scene where the least activity occurred, thus the place where the least evidence is located. This is the safe pathway.
2. Ensure, *really ensure*, that everyone, *literally everyone*, follows the safe pathway. Identifying the safe pathway and then allowing higher-ranking officers to push their weight around and violate proper crime scene protocol is ludicrous.

EMTs and firefighters called to aid the victim worry about the life of the victim and will cross through the middle of the crime scene unless instructed to follow the safe pathway. Under most circumstances, these EMTs and firefighters will follow the officer's request to protect the evidence and follow the safe pathway.

Having said this, throw all of it out the window if a human life hangs in the balance. Saving a life overrides all concerns about protecting the integrity of evidence, regardless of what other crime scene "experts" say. Imagine your child, or anyone you love, lying injured and waiting for help. Imagine a police officer trying to direct foot traffic through a crime scene while your loved one gasps for life. This picture is wrong, and it should never happen. Save the life first. Protect the evidence later. But when conditions allow, the safe pathway is perhaps the best way to ensure that the majority of crime scene evidence remains protected.

I have a message for those high-ranking officers who respond to major crime scenes: *Stay the hell out!* There is nothing you can do to help that CSI. Trust the investigation to the officers you have identified and entrusted as crime scene investigators. Here are three common arguments I've heard and my responses to them:

- "But I gotta see!" No, you don't. Get the info later from the people trained to examine the crime scene.
- "But I know what I'm doing." So what? You don't belong in the crime scene and your presence is the bad kind of contamination.
- "But I got rank." Then show you've earned it by respecting the crime scene and staying out.

In the Troy Barboza murder, his crime scene was crawling with ranking officers—those officers with ranks above lieutenant and not attached to the CSI. They were gathered on the patio, the same place the killer stood when he shot and killed Barboza. They also walked about the interior of the crime scene, presumably to look over his body. To add to the contamination, they brought a police chaplain into the crime scene to pray over his body. With all due respect, that was completely inappropriate.

A big problem with protecting the crime scene is that usually the officer with the least seniority is given the task of standing at the crime scene post. Here is the new guy in the department who is confronted by ranking officers who immediately proceed to violate the principles of crime scene protection. And the new guy is apt to smile gracefully as the older, ranking officers push past him. Rank has its privileges. And too many times, senior ranking officers will ignore the advice and requests of the investigating team to remain outside the crime scene. They'll walk in, look, touch, and put themselves in places they ought not to be, then walk out with no thought whatsoever to submitting a written report about their activities in the crime scene. It's a sad state of affairs. But Hawai'i is not alone in dealing with this problem. I've spoken to many homicide investigators from other states who identify this problem as something they, too, have a difficult time dealing with.

Evidence, You Say?

Okay, so an officer has done everything to protect the crime scene and its evidence. But what is "evidence"? There is a very simple but formal definition that police officers need to remember. Evidence can be (1) anything that (2) establishes guilt or innocence, (3) provided it can be legally presented in court.

"Anything" speaks for itself. "Establishes guilt or innocence" has been a bit difficult for some officers to swallow at times. When they're absolutely certain that Joe Blow committed a crime but then learn something that shows Mr. Blow did not commit that crime, their pride can be hurt. It is human nature to want to ignore those items of evidence that prove Mr. Blow was innocent.

"What do you mean we're on the wrong track? Joe Blow is guilty, damn it!"

"Is he?"

What happens next is that those officers will expend a great deal of effort to disprove the evidence that exonerates Joe Blow—many times failing to do so. Being completely neutral is a critically important trait that a criminal investigator must have. Without that, innocent people can go to jail.

And "provided it (the evidence) can be legally presented" means that police obey the laws set down by constitutions and courts. It sounds simple enough. Yet so often, police bend and twist those laws and rules to fit their needs. Remember the concept of integrity. It's better to do things properly than be caught and looked upon as a law enforcement official with no values.

There are more formal definitions that apply to evidence. Here are some examples:

Real (or Physical) Evidence
This is evidence that has width, breadth, and depth. But we must remember that microscopic items also fall into this category.

Testimonial Evidence
This is evidence in the form of a statement. A few conditions are attached to this form of evidence.

1. The witness who provided the statement must, in the majority of cases, be available to provide the testimony in court. Under a few conditions, the witness's statement may *not* be admissible in court; one example is that the witness has died. In that case, a judge may allow a detective to read the dead person's statement.
2. A dying declaration may be admitted, but other conditions must exist: (a) the person giving the statement must believe he or she is dying, and (b) the person must die.

Real and testimonial evidence can also occur in either of the two following forms:

Direct Evidence
This is evidence that directly proves a fact. For example, a bullet

removed from a victim's body is compared with a bullet test-fired from a suspect's gun, and they match. The only thing directly proved is that the victim was shot by that gun, not who fired it.

Circumstantial Evidence

This is evidence that requires interpretation by a judge or jury. Using the scenario above, the prosecution will attempt to convince the jury that the suspect fired the gun, based on, perhaps, the person's proximity to the offense when caught and gunpowder residue on the hands. The defense will argue that the suspect was given the weapon by a friend and the gunpowder was a result of firing another gun earlier while shooting at pigeons with other friends.

We'll see in the following chapters that evidence can literally be anything. The criminal investigator must understand that evidence, from fingerprints to microscopic particles, *will* be at a crime scene. It's his job to find it. And knowledge of forensic procedures will help him do just that.

The Basics

There are three basic things that crime scene investigators must do at each major crime scene. Then it seems that a thousand other things need to be done. But these three basics must be done first. Every major crime scene will require some form of each of these elements.

Searches

A search of the crime scene is required in every case. The degree of detail of that search depends on the severity of the crime. What becomes important is that in each case a particular type of search may be required. All officers and crime scene technicians should know the different types of searches and when they should be used. Unfortunately, the most commonly used search is the "look around a little bit" method. Sadly, too many officers consider a search to be simply looking around the scene for something that may tie into the crime.

My homicide team spoke to an officer once who said that he already searched the scene. "What did you do?" we asked. He answered, "I looked around; neva' find anything."

This won't do. Searches are much more than merely looking around. They even have names.

The Line Search

The name of this search describes it well. The technician or officer must walk the scene—slowly—in a line looking for evidence. As he walks, he looks at the ground in front of him. If he turns his head from side to side he misses observation of the ground on the opposite side from where he's looking. So a searcher should never look at a space on the ground wider than three feet, so that he never has to turn his head. The searcher simply walks in a straight line, as best he can, and when he reaches the end, moves over a couple of feet and walks back. After finishing this pattern, the technician moves perpendicular to the line pattern and does it again, crisscrossing the previously walked lines.

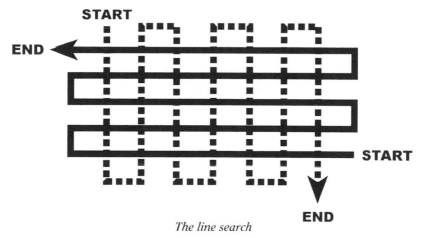

The line search

The Grid Search

Again, this search is exactly as its name implies. The crime scene is simply divided into grids, and each grid is line-searched separately. Usually this pattern is reserved for indoor scenes. Each cell of the

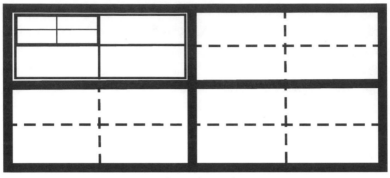

The grid search

grid can be divided again, making for a smaller search area. The searchers then move from grid to grid until all areas are completely searched.

The spiral search

The Spiral Search

How convenient can the name of this search pattern be? Start at the outside and spiral in to the center. An exception is at a bomb explosion crime scene, which starts at the seat of the explosion and then moves outward until no more evidence is found.

The Zone Search

This search is the outdoor version of the indoor grid search. There is no great mystery here. The crime scene is divided into zones, which are not neatly defined by the walls of an indoor scene.

As with the indoor scene, the zones can be subdivided and line-searched until the entire area is completely inspected.

Photography

Crime scene photography isn't quite the same as taking pictures at a family reunion. There are specific types of photos that must be taken because they will tell a story and corroborate the crime scene as described in the investigator's report and diagrams. In major cases, it is not uncommon for the crime scene photographer to take as many as three or four hundred photos. From these photos, the investigator will select those that most accurately describe the scene and the evidence. The remaining photos are saved in a file and can be made available to the defense attorneys should they wish to see them. There are four types of photos that need to be taken.

Area/Location Photos

These photos depict where in the city or town the crime scene is located. Normally the photographer takes photos of the street where the crime scene is located, looking in both directions, and if possible the street sign identifying the name of the street. Included in these area photos will be one of the scene from across the street. Ideally, this photo will include a mailbox or something that carries the house number.

The area photos may include aerial photography. This helps pinpoint the crime scene in the city, town, or specific location of the scene. A crime scene photographer goes up in the agency's helicopter, flying over the scene, and takes photos as close to vertical as possible. The helicopter must make banking turns to allow the photographer to get vertical shots. This can have unfortunate and potentially disastrous results.

In one murder investigation, the crime scene photographer went up in a helicopter to take aerial photos. He was strapped tightly into the seat and held his photography equipment bag on his lap. The helicopter had open-air doors in the shape of a large oval. As the copter neared the crime scene site, the pilot made sure that the photographer was strapped in securely and was ready to take the photos. He then turned the copter into a bank, allowing the photographer to photograph the scene from a nearly 90-degree angle. It was then that the photographer learned a valuable lesson: Never leave the photography equipment bag loose on your lap. The bag, containing costly cameras, lenses, and other supplies, slid from his lap and out of the helicopter. *Swoosh*—they were gone. Luckily, no one on the ground was injured by the falling bag. But the same can't be said for the equipment.

Witness/Observation Photos

These photos are different from the area photos in that they are much closer to the scene itself and show the immediate vicinity of the crime scene as observed by someone onsite. Examples are a house from a driveway, the hallway leading to a classroom door, and the view into a scene from just outside its perimeter. It was our practice to have the photographer stand just inside the scene and take photos, slightly overlapping each other, until a 360-degree panoramic view was obtained.

Evidence Photos

This type of photo speaks for itself. An evidence photo from various angles should be taken of any item that can be considered evidence. Such photos need to be pristine—that is, without anything in the photo that was added by the photo technician, such as rulers and report numbers.

Close-up Photos

Close-up photos are identical to evidence photos except that a six-inch ruler is added close to the object being photographed to show size.

Videotaping

Attitudes concerning videotaping vary among both police and

prosecutors. Video offers a more active picture of the crime scene than still photography, but as with still photography, it can be argued that videotaping is the selective view of the photographer.

One major question is whether to videotape with or without sound. And if sound is chosen, is it narrated by the photographer, or does it simply contain background noise? A big concern is recording the ambient conversations of investigators and technicians at the crime scene. To eliminate this, it is advisable to remove all persons from the crime scene until the videotaping is done. But this also leaves the scene open to contamination while it's being taped.

There are no easy answers, but my experience as the lieutenant-in-charge of the Homicide Detail was that taping was a big pain in the derrière. We videotaped one murder scene in Pearl City, and because everyone was busy, I volunteered to be the video photographer. We chose to use narration, and I was giving a blow-by-blow account of what I could see through the viewfinder. Keep in mind that we did not have the small palm-size camcorders used today. We used the big eighteen-inch, shoulder-mounted model that had only an eyepiece. In documenting the exterior of the victim's house, I walked along the side of the garage to the gate leading to the backyard. I opened the gate and turned left. Through the eyepiece, I saw a very large dog that looked at me and clearly said, "Lunch!" Later, when we viewed the tape, we saw the picture go completely *kapakahi* and heard my string of obscenities directed at the dog.

Diagrams

Like photography, diagrams help to document the crime scene. They refresh witnesses' and detectives' memories about the scene and they complement photography to represent the best means of scene documentation. Different types of diagrams are used, depending on what needs to be documented.

There are certain requirements for the drawings. In major crimes, the diagrams must be to scale. This means that the drawing will show that one-quarter of an inch equals one foot. The lines on common graph paper already have these dimensions. Somewhere on the drawing should be an arrow showing the direction of north. It's not necessary to show south, east, and west.

Here's a cute trick to play with your family. Get everyone together, the more the merrier. Weddings work great for this, and never mind the objections of the bride—she'll get over it. Ask everyone to close their eyes and when you say "Go," have them point in the direction they think is north. I do this with my classes, and nearly everyone points in a different direction. Sadly but inevitably, someone will point straight up! This little exercise is proof that people who do crime scene drawings need a compass.

Each drawing also needs a legend. The legend system can be either numbers or letters, but it should remain consistent and not flip-flop back and forth.

At crime scenes, drawings are made in the rough and the final diagram is completed at headquarters. To speed things up, a second person assists the technician doing the draft drawing. This guy usually has the least to do and ends up at the "stupid" end of the tape. He hears the same words a lot: "Hold the end of the tape here" or "Hold the end of the tape there," over and over again. I was often asked to hold the end of the tape. I considered it an honor even if the word "stupid" was attached to it.

Evidentiary items in the crime scene must be "placed" in the drawing, and this is done by measuring the distance to one permanent wall, then to another perpendicular one. Where the two lines intersect is the location of the evidence. This is important because courts at times like to return to the scenes and actually place evidence where it was originally found.

The Floor Plan Diagram

This diagram represents the crime scene as if you removed the roof and were looking straight down into the building. It's the easiest and most common diagram, but it can be tedious, as all items of evidence must be placed in the drawing. This drawing is literally a

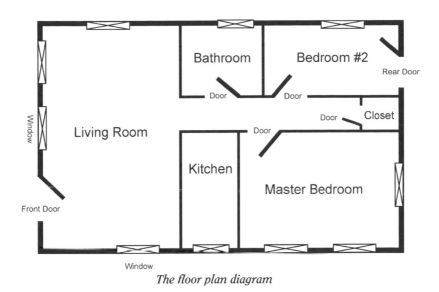

The floor plan diagram

floor plan diagram such as that used to decorate a home or plan an addition.

The elevation diagram

The Elevation Diagram

The elevation diagram has the same requirements as the floor plan diagram except that the drawing is of a wall; it shows a vertical portion of the scene instead of a horizontal one, as would be depicted in the floor plan diagram.

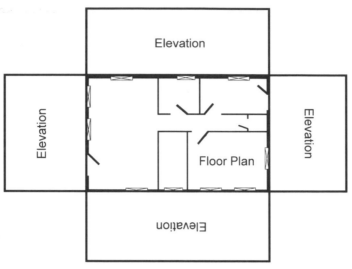

The exploded view diagram

The Exploded View Diagram

This diagram contains elements of both the floor plan and elevation diagrams. The result is similar to taking a cardboard box and cutting the corners of the box from top to bottom, leaving it attached to the bottom at the fold. The important feature here is that the four elevation drawings, which are now lying flat, must be drawn in relation to how they would look standing up as walls.

The perspective diagram

The Perspective Diagram

The most difficult of the four drawings, the perspective diagram is the least used. Because angles and degrees of slope are necessary, such drawings are used primarily in negligent homicide cases, when the traffic investigators use instruments that are similar to surveying equipment.

Software Programs

Today there are software programs that create diagrams. However, the rough drawing at the scene still needs to be made, after which the information is manually entered into a computer. These are called computer-aided design (CAD) programs. They can be highly efficient, providing the crime scene technician with a very large array of individual items found in and around homes and other buildings, such as chairs, tables, beds, lamps, kitchen items, garage items, trees, and foliage.

The programs also provide the means to create the walls, doors, and windows seen in the floor plan diagrams. The one major drawback, in my view, is that such diagrams lack the human touch, and they really look like computer drawings. In the early 1990s, when I was in charge of the Scientific Investigation Section, which was responsible for CSIs, we conducted a little informal experiment: we compared a CAD drawing with a drawing made by a human hand. There was no contest. The computer won. But, again in my judgment, the drawing composed by the evidence tech "looked" better. It was softer and seemed to have life to it. But the computer was faster.

A Final Word

While you don't have to be an expert at math (thank you, Lord!), drawings can be intensely tedious and in some cases difficult, as with the Troy Barboza case discussed at length in *Honolulu Homicide*. The technicians in Barboza's murder investigation were required to submit various styles of drawings to accurately represent the scene.

But crime scene technicians need to be much more than just artists. They need to be photographers. They need to be as inquisitive as Sherlock Holmes. And they need to have a burning fire in their heart to do the best they can to find the evidence at the scene that will identify the criminal.

Crime Scene Experiment #1: Center of Balance

Follow the steps exactly.

Find a wall in your home near a door frame. Make sure that there are no items of furniture near it. Have a partner stand near you as you approach the wall. Put the side of your right foot against the wall. Make sure that the whole side of your foot is touching the wall at the ground. Put your right shoulder against the wall and have the side of your right leg, right arm, and torso touch the wall. Bring your left leg in toward the wall.

You can't do it, can you? That's because your center of gravity is too far left. What did you do when you moved your left foot toward the wall? Did you reach out and grab the door frame to prevent yourself from falling? Or did you just fall into your partner's arms?

If you didn't lose your balance, you cheated, you crook!

Crime Scene Experiment #2: Crime Scene Diagram

Equipment:
1. Pencil
2. Eraser
3. Graph paper or plain white paper
4. Tape rule
5. A partner to help you hold the "stupid" end of the tape rule

Step 1: Choose a room in your house. Draw a rough outline of the room. Begin at a corner of your choosing and measure the wall to the next interruption, such as a door frame or window frame. Log the distance in inches on your rough drawing. Continue these measurements until you have completely encircled your room.

Step 2: On separate sheets, draw a rough outline of each wall. Take measurements of the various interruptions on the wall (doors and windows) from the interruption to the floor, then to the ceiling.

Step 3: After you have logged all your measurements, sit down with a clean piece of graph paper and draw out your diagram (with straight lines) of an exploded view of your room.

Step 4 (optional): Grab a box of crayons and create a masterpiece.

2
Fingerprints

The use of fingerprints as a criminal investigative tool is known to nearly everyone. You hear of fingerprint evidence in the movies, you read of it in mystery novels. If you have ever been a victim of a burglary, the police officer who comes to your house looks for them. But there is much more to fingerprints than that simple realization.

What Are Fingerprints?

Fingerprints are ridges of skin called "friction ridges." They are formed during the embryo stage in humans, and they remain unchanged (naturally) until death. Decomposition is the only natural way that fingerprints change their shape. These friction ridges form on our fingers and palms and the soles and toes of our feet. Fingerprints are unique to every person. No two people have ever been found to have identical fingerprints.

Fingerprints are one way to identify people—in many cases, people accused of committing a crime. The individual characteristics of these friction ridges are classified in what is known as the Henry System of Fingerprint Classification.

A Little Bit of Identification History

In 1883 a French police expert, Alphonse Bertillon, devised an identification system for criminal suspects that revolved around detailed physical descriptions. Bertillon's method rested on his belief that the dimensions of the human body remained fixed from the age of twenty until death. He believed that skeleton sizes were so diverse that no two individuals could have exactly the same measurements. Bertillon recommended routinely taking eleven measurements of

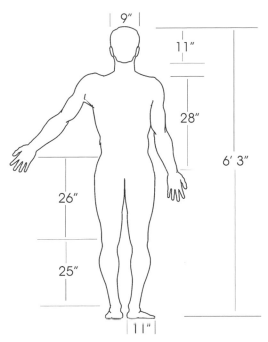

The Bertillon System

the human body. The major and most important of these measurements were a person's height, reach, width of the head, and length of the left foot. From 1882 to the end of the century, the Bertillon System was considered the most accurate method of identification.

In 1892 François Galton published a book on fingerprints and their obvious differences, intended as a supplement to the Bertillon System. But in 1897 Sir Edward Richard Henry devised the fingerprint classification system that is still used in law enforcement today.

The Bertillon System came to an end in 1903 when a convicted felon, one Will West, was sent to Leavenworth Prison. When he arrived he was confronted by the warden, who welcomed him back. West denied ever having been to Leavenworth. Measurements were taken of him using the Bertillon System, and they matched those on file for a William West. Will West protested. Upon further checks, the astonished warden learned that convicted murderer William West was already confined in Leavenworth—and he had the identical measurements of the newly arrived Will West. The Bertillon System went out the window and the Henry Fingerprint Classification System became widely used.

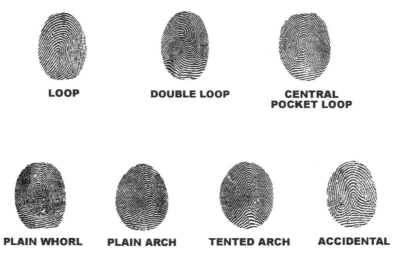

LOOP   DOUBLE LOOP   CENTRAL
                                   POCKET LOOP

PLAIN WHORL   PLAIN ARCH   TENTED ARCH   ACCIDENTAL

When the police search crime scenes for prints, they are looking for evidence of Henry's seven different classifications of fingerprints. Prints come in the following three types:

1. *Plastic fingerprints.* These are fingerprints left in pliable material such as painter's putty. The material is firm enough in its elastic nature to retain the fingerprint. Examples of common, everyday pliable substances are Silly Putty, partially dried oil-based paint, soft cheese, and peanut butter (my favorite food).

2. *Foreign-matter fingerprints.* These are fingerprints made with a foreign substance and left on a surface, such as a fingerprint stained with blood. Other common examples of foreign matter are wet paint, ink, and mud.

3. *Latent fingerprints.* This is the most common type of fingerprint left at crime scenes. "Latent" means "hidden." It's

sometimes sitting there in plain sight, but it can't really be seen. This type of print is made up of the oils and acids that we exude from our bodies, usually through perspiration that accumulates on our hands. We can add oils to our hands by touching our face, making in some cases very good latent prints just waiting to be recovered. Because latent prints are difficult to see without some form of aid, care should be taken to locate and properly recover them for future analysis.

How Are Prints Recovered?

There are many different ways to recover latent prints. The following are but a few of the more common means used by crime scene analysts.

Powders and Brushes

The most frequently used method of recovering latent fingerprints is to dust surfaces with graphite powder, then to "recover" the print onto a plain white index card.

The tools for this technique are rather simple. The powder is a fine dust made of graphite, which is "dusted" onto a surface using a brush. Brushes come in different forms. When I entered the department in 1971, we were issued feather brushes. These were made of soft feathers that were pulled apart to enhance their downy texture. The drawback was that they were expensive.

They are even more expensive today and difficult to get, and I wish I had had the foresight to keep the one issued to me. The brush used by most officers today is made of soft nylon fibers and is fairly inexpensive.

But both feather and nylon brushes have one drawback: As soft as they may seem, they are both firm enough that if they are rubbed too hard they may actually damage the print. An alternative is a device called a magna-brush. It's not a brush at all, but rather a magnet in a penlike shape. The magna-brush uses a special graphite

Nylon and magna brushes

powder that contains fine metal shavings. The shavings cling to the end of the magna-brush, holding a clump of powder with them. With this device, only the powder touches the print, reducing the chance of damaging the latent.

In addition to the graphite powder, fluorescent powders are used in conjunction with strong lights or lasers to assist in locating the latent print. The fluorescence of the powder highlights the latent when it is hit with a laser, and the crime scene investigator can then mark that latent for recovery.

Powders also come in different colors. It makes little sense to dust a black object with black graphite powder, and so forth. The different-colored powders help investigators in dusting a variety of colored objects.

Photography
Photography is probably the next most common method of recovering fingerprints. But the photo needs to be on a 1:1 basis. This will allow the identification technician to view the print as it

exists in real life. Then, if necessary, the item that is holding the print can itself be physically recovered. In the Barboza murder, we found a print on a wooden surface, which we felt was so important that we cut the wooden piece away and brought it in.

Superglue

The use of superglue in law enforcement evolved accidentally when a Japanese scientist used it in a closed container and learned that the superglue fumes highlighted fingerprints.

Superglue is used whenever there is an object that is difficult to dust with powders. The object is placed into a container similar to a fish tank, and superglue is placed on a small lidlike container and inserted into the tank on top of a heating device such as a light bulb. The cover of the tank is put on and sealed tightly. The light bulb is turned on, and the resulting heat evaporates the superglue and produces fumes. The fumes cover any object in the tank, and any fingerprints there are coated a grayish-white color. The prints can then be photographed on a 1:1 basis and recovered.

Occasionally, larger areas are superglued as well. I have been present when our evidence technicians superglued the interior of a

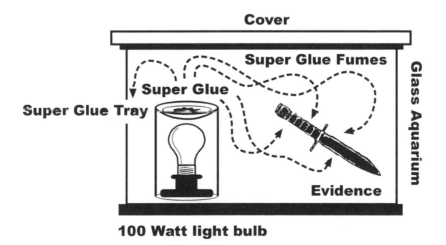

A typical super glue tank

vehicle. Small containers of superglue are placed inside the car at various points atop heating devices such as "canned heat." The car openings are sealed. Several hours later, the inside of the vehicle is coated with the gray film and the search for prints begins.

By the way, a more challenging way to describe this process is "cyanoacrylate fuming." I prefer "superglue."

Fingerprints from Paper

Fingerprints on paper can be recovered simply by dusting the paper. This is not the preferred way, however, as it leaves the paper dirty and there is a risk that the print can smear. The preferred method to recover prints from paper is to use the chemical liquid ninhydrin. The paper items are dipped in the ninhydrin solution. As they dry, any fingerprints on the items will appear and will be stained purple. Unfortunately, these prints will also disappear with time, so photography is the method used to "recover" them. There is one other drawback in the use of ninhydrin. It is carcinogenic, so it must be used under strict laboratory conditions, employing a hooded vent that sucks the fumes out and away from the person processing the prints.

Latent Prints on a Human Body

It is also possible to obtain fingerprints left on a human body by a suspect. There are different ways to do this, and there are several factors involved in these processes. The first is whether the victim is alive or dead. If the victim is dead, the prints may last longer due simply to the fact that a living victim may perspire, which could ruin the print. Another factor is the environment and weather conditions. A victim outside will be exposed to the weather, which will reduce the time that the print may be recoverable. Yet another factor is whether or not the victim is hairy. The more hair, the less chance there is of finding fingerprints.

Skin suspected of having prints can be dusted just like any other surface. But this creates the problem of dirtying the skin with the powder itself. This problem arose in a case in the late 1980s in which the nude body of a woman was dumped in the brush alongside a roadway on Windward Oʻahu. Since she appeared to have been dead for only a very short period of time and had apparently been raped, her body was a good candidate for immediate dusting for prints. The medical examiner (ME) objected. The dust would interfere with his ability to view the body free of outside contamination. We knew, however, that her body would be wrapped in a sheet, placed in a plastic body bag, and placed in a refrigerator. The cold would cause condensation to cover the body, ruining any possibility of obtaining fingerprints. We decided that the importance of obtaining the prints outweighed dirtying the body with the dust. Sadly, we were not able to obtain any latent prints—and we really angered the ME.

Lasers and Other Light Sources

It's common knowledge that high-intensity light is a great aid in locating latent fingerprints. Holding a strong light at an oblique

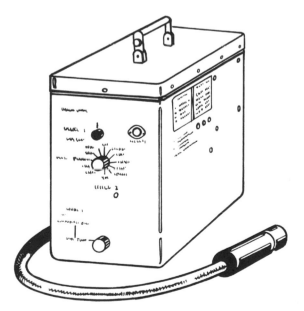

A portable laser unit

angle helps illuminate a fingerprint that may otherwise be missed in normal light. There are several high-intensity lights that can be used by police agencies. The first and most common is the laser. "Laser" is an acronym for "light amplification by stimulated emission of radiation." Most police agencies have portable laser units that can be taken to crime scenes and larger tabletop models that can be used on evidence recovered and brought to the police station. Another strong light source is the high-intensity arc lamp that many agencies have in addition to lasers. In either case, the cost of this equipment is high.

Safety is also a concern. Lasers used improperly can injure people at crime scenes. Eye protection is an absolute must. When a laser was used in an indoor scene, our practice in the 1980s and 1990s was to remove all persons from the room other than the technicians using the laser and marking the prints for later recovery. Safety in investigations is paramount.

Other Ways of Recovering Prints

Another way of recovering prints is iodine fuming. Iodine is one of the oldest substances used to locate latent prints on porous surfaces such as skin, but it is also toxic.

Because prints are left from the oils on our fingers, it is also possible to obtain prints from skin by transferring them to absorbent paper, such as that used to absorb facial oils. The paper, if wrapped around a solid block and pressed against the skin, may absorb the oily fingerprint. The paper is then subjected to various techniques to locate latent prints.

Yet another way to locate prints on water-soaked items is to use a small-particle reagent (SPR) such as molybdenum disulfide (say that six times fast). SPR is normally sprayed on the wet item and adheres to the prints on nonporous surfaces.

Submitting the Print

Once the investigators have dusted items and located prints, the next trick is to lift the prints off their surfaces. This is done by applying a special fingerprint-lifting tape onto the print, carefully pulling it off, and laying it on a clean white index card.

Regardless of how prints are recovered, the key issue is that they are handled extremely carefully. Fingerprint comparison is still the best way to identify a suspect, and crime scene analysts cannot be careless with latent prints or they might lose the one critical piece of evidence they need to identify and convict the suspect.

How Long Does a Print Last?

People may not believe that prints can last an extremely long time, but it's true—to a certain extent. It depends on a number of factors: the environment, the surface where the print was left, and the type of print that was left. For example, a fingerprint left in painter's putty that is indoors and out of the weather could last as long as the painter's putty lasts. Another example is a blood-contaminated finger that lays down a fingerprint on a smooth surface, then dries. If it's indoors, away from the elements, it also could last a very, very long time.

But a latent print composed of body oils and left on the outside of a car that is used every day will not last very long. The sun, rain, dew, dust and dirt, and flying debris from the roadway could very soon obliterate that latent print.

What About Gloves?

I once taught a weekly Department of Education TV special that focused on forensic science. In one segment we talked about fingerprints, and I mentioned that even if the crooks are wearing gloves, it is possible to recover latent prints.

One particular police major went ballistic. He screamed at me, his spittle flying in all directions. "What the hell are you doing? You're giving away our secrets! Now the crooks will know that we can get prints even if they're wearing gloves."

After I wiped my face dry, I explained that first of all, very few crooks would be watching a local school science series on TV.

Second, there are movies, TV shows, and specials that tell all about forensic science and criminal investigations. Finally, it is well known in police circles that the majority of petty crooks can be told one minute that "we can get your fingerprints even if you wear gloves" and the next minute commit their crime without gloves at all and leave beautiful latent prints at the crime scene.

Some crooks wear thin latex rubber gloves—the kind used by your doctor in an exam. These gloves "breathe." After a while, the hands become sweaty. Before the crook knows it, the glove begins to exude the oils from his hands. What the crook also doesn't know is the fact that the glove conforms to all the friction ridges of his fingerprints. When the crook touches something, he leaves his latent fingerprint on the surface he touched.

Some crooks use gloves to commit their crime and, satisfied that they're home free, pull off the gloves and toss them in the rubbish can. If the police can find those gloves, they may get lucky and recover beautiful fingerprints left by the crook on the inside of the glove.

Let's assume the crook knows that latex gloves don't truly protect him from leaving fingerprints at crime scenes, so he goes out and buys leather gloves. What he forgets is that leather is the skin of some animal, usually some poor cow who gave his all for the dinner table. Well, that cow can rest in peace knowing that his hide was saved, tanned, and sewn into very comfortable gloves that some crooks use. What the crook does not realize is that the cow's skin pattern on leather gloves can be left at crime scenes. These can also be recovered. And if the cops can catch the crook, and if the crook still has the leather gloves on his person, then the skin pattern on those gloves can be compared with the leather skin pattern recovered from the crime scene.

A Final Word

We really don't have crooks who are that stupid, do we? So the crook reads this book and goes out and buys cotton gloves. That'll show those cops, huh? Guess what? The weave pattern of the cotton fiber that the glove was made of can be compared to the weave pattern of the cotton fiber left at the crime scene exactly as the leather skin pattern can be compared.

But I got a ton of grief (to put it politely) from one elderly captain who shook his head, absolutely believing that we would soon have series after series of burglaries all over the island. We spoke aloud the secrets that only cops knew.

"That's how we caught the crooks," he said. "The crooks didn't know our secrets."

"But, Captain, I was speaking to police recruits."

"You never know who they know. You don't know if they're going home and telling their cousin who's a crook. Dias, what you doing?"

"Teaching our young recruits."

So if you're a crook, go ahead and read this book. I bet in a day or so, you'll be leaving your fingerprints all over the scene—even while you're wearing gloves.

Gotcha!

Fingerprint Experiment #1: Fingerprint Classification

Get a washable marker. Go ahead, take it from your kid—we won't tell. Working quickly to prevent the ink from drying, rub the palm side of your fingertips with the washable marker. Then using the chart on the next page (or your own chart, if you don't like mine), press each finger onto its respective square. Ink and press only one finger at a time, or the ink may dry. Press straight down gently. For this experiment, do not roll your fingers, as you may have seen police officers do. After you have taken your own "inked prints," check back with the chart on page 24. Using that chart, classify your own fingerprints. It's okay to use a magnifying glass. We won't consider it cheating.

Fingerprint Classification of

(Name):_____

Right Thumb Classification				
Right Index Classification	Left Thumb Classification			
Right Middle Classification	Left Index Classification			
Right Ring Classification	Left Middle Classification			
Right Pinky Classification	Left Ring Classification			
	Left Pinky Classification			

Fingerprint Experiment #2: Locating Fingerprints via Superglue Technique

Equipment:

1. Quart-size mayonnaise jar with lid
2. 2" x 2" square of aluminum foil
3. 2" x 4" rectangle of aluminum foil
4. Tube of superglue
5. Tweezers

Clean the mayonnaise jar. Fold up one-eighth inch of the sides of the 2" x 2" aluminum foil to make a small square dish. Place this piece of foil onto the inside bottom of the mayonnaise jar. Take the 2" x 4" rectangle of aluminum foil and set it on a flat, firm surface. Press your fingers onto the rectangle. If you have oily fingers, you may actually see your latent fingerprints. That's okay. Take the superglue tube and open it according to its instructions. Carefully drop six to eight drops of superglue onto the square aluminum dish at the bottom of the mayonnaise jar. Using tweezers, place the aluminum rectangle into the mayonnaise jar, being careful to avoid placing it into the aluminum square that's holding the superglue. Screw the cover onto the mayonnaise jar and carefully place it in a location where it will not be disturbed. Wait twenty-four hours.

When you open the jar, don't breathe in the fumes. Give the jar a few minutes to air out; then, using the tweezers, pull out the aluminum rectangle. You should see that the evaporating superglue fumes have coated your fingerprints with a white or grayish film.

If it didn't work, you must have done something wrong. Follow instructions next time!

Fingerprint Experiment #3: Obtaining Fingerprints from Skin

Equipment:

1. Smooth block of wood about 3" wide x 5" long x 2" thick
2. Several sheets of absorbent tissue paper (used to help remove facial oils); if you don't have this, regular tissue paper can be used

3. Human volunteer with smooth, hairless skin
4. One container of women's facial or bath powder, preferably powder that is colored
5. Women's powder brush

You may wish to cheat a little here and ensure that your fingers are just a little bit oily. Place a few latent fingerprints on the smooth, hairless skin of your volunteer. Where that skin is located on your volunteer's body is your choice, with the consent of the volunteer, of course. Press firmly onto the skin.

Take a sheet of absorbent tissue paper and wrap it snugly around the smooth wooden block. Press the block firmly against the skin of your volunteer where you laid down the fingerprints, and hold it there for twenty to thirty seconds. Remove the paper and set it on a smooth, dry surface.

Very carefully "dust" the paper with the powder. The powder should cling to the fingerprint oils absorbed onto the tissue paper.

If it didn't work, you must have done something wrong again, or something's wrong with your skin; go see a dermatologist!

3
Trace Evidence

The term "trace evidence" is used to describe any small items of evidence. It's rather a generic term, because it signifies a variety of objects, excluding primarily serological and fingerprint evidence. It can often be tiny items that an investigator might miss on first examination. It can also be microscopic items that can be seen only with the aid of a microscope. In many instances, trace evidence has proved to be the means of solving the case—of identifying a suspect or connecting the suspect to the victim. This was demonstrated dramatically in 1982 in the case of Wayne Williams in Atlanta, Georgia.

In 1982 Atlanta was a city terrorized by a serial killer. The bodies of many young black boys and teens were discovered. They had been strangled or smothered, apparently by the same person. The police were stymied, and the cases were the leading news stories of the time. This fact led to the belief that the killer was following police activity through the media. For example, when the information was released that the police had discovered hair and fibers on several victims, bodies began to show up in rivers and ponds, just as the FBI had predicted. This suggests the killer believed that water would wash away the evidence. Following this lead, police found Wayne Williams, a self-employed music producer, on a bridge over the river where a body was dumped. Hair and fibers taken from the victims matched fibers from Williams's home and car and hair from his dog. Williams was arrested, charged, and convicted on multiple murders.

Trace evidence is based on the scientific theory known as the Locard Exchange Principle. Thank God it is physics and not math. (Math and I declared war on each other during my junior year in high school when my trigonometry teacher, with the largest and

"Watch where you're going"

Locard Exchange Principle

most sinister grin he could muster, informed me that I had flunked his class and would have to retake it during the summer or I would not join my fellow classmates in the fall.)

French scientist Edmund Locard developed his now famous theory of transfer in 1928. It simply states that *when two objects come into contact with each other, a partial transfer of material occurs and each object leaves evidence of its presence on the other.* An example of this would be the imprint of my father's wedding ring on the side of my head when he learned that I flunked that trig course, and the hairs from my head that collected under his ring. He would have been convicted easily.

Sources of Trace Evidence

Trace evidence can come from nearly any object that you can think of, using Locard's principle as a foundation of understanding. There are, however, some major categories of sources that police investigators consider when looking for trace evidence.

Clothing

Clothing often provides an excellent source of trace evidence because of the fibers that fall from it. Footwear is equally important, because small items tend to cling to the soles of shoes, sandals, and slippers. Fibers and evidence on the bottom of shoes can tie a suspect to a crime scene.

The Human Body

A tremendous amount of evidence can be recovered from a human body. In crimes in which there is physical contact between suspect and victim, the possibility is great that an exchange of items between the two people will occur. Often the victim will scratch an assailant, particularly during assault and sexual offenses. It then becomes important to recover the fingernail scrapings from the victim and the suspect. Hair transfer between victim and suspect is also very likely. Careful examination of the bodies of both the victim and the suspect is important.

In cases where a firearm has been used, it is necessary to attempt to recover gunshot residue from the hands of the suspect. This exam is also known as the GSR analysis. One particularly good examination for evidence from a human body is a test known mostly by its initials: TMDT, or trace metal detection test. This involves a chemical solution of 8-hydroxyquinoline prepared in isopropanol. This solution is sprayed on human skin to see if a hand recently held a weapon or whether a weapon was placed in a suspect's waistband. In training classes at Ke Kula Makai police academy during the late 1980s and early 1990s, we routinely had a recruit begin the day by wearing a revolver in his waistband. Later in the afternoon, we sprayed the belly of this recruit with TMDT. In nearly every instance, the recruit's skin showed the outline of the revolver, including the frame, the cylinder, and the barrel.

In murder cases, in fact, the body of the victim should be considered a crime scene in and of itself, as it may reveal a great amount of information and evidence. Examination for trace evidence, therefore, must be a procedure that takes every possibility into account.

Other Items

Tools and weapons used in the commission of a crime are also sources of trace evidence. Tools used in burglaries, for example, may contain evidence of the surface upon which they were used, yielding samples of paint, glass, or wood. A hammer, normally considered a tool, may contain hair from a victim when it is used as a weapon. The hammer used to kill State Representative Roland Kotani, described in *Honolulu Homicide,* probably had on it his hair as well as his blood. This was never confirmed. The killer, in an attempt to hide her identity, threw the hammer away before Kotani's body was found. Other weapons such as knives and guns may also hold hair and fibers.

Can guns hold evidence? Yes, they can, when used under certain conditions. For example, a gun held against a victim's head or at very close range and then fired may actually have traces of blood, hair, skin, and bone on it or in its barrel. This is a result of a circumstance known as "blowback," which occurs when high-velocity blood spatter blows back from the wound toward the gun and shooter.

Examples of Trace Evidence

Trace evidence can be just about anything. The word "trace" implies that the object wouldn't be the size of an elephant. Trace evidence is something that doesn't call attention to itself. It is something that needs to be searched for. And this is the aspect of a CSI that can create problems, depending on how it is conducted. Because of the Locard Theory, we can say that no matter the crime or the crime scene, there *will* be evidence at the scene; it's the job of the investigator and technicians *to find it.*

There are some common items that investigators and technicians look for when searching crime scenes for small objects. The following is not a complete list, but it includes those items that have generally been found at various crime scenes.

Paint Chips

These can range from large pieces to extremely small scrapings of dried paint from some surface, particularly at locations where entry into a building was forced. If such paint chips can be found on a suspect or a tool that the suspect has, there is the possibility that a comparison can be made with the paint from the crime scene. In addition to a simple comparison, paint, varnish, and other lacquer finishes can be identified and also compared via their chemical properties.

One important factor in looking at paint is the layering aspect. If you live in an older house, it's quite possible that it has several layers of paint, perhaps even layers of different colors. This can be seen even more readily with automobile paint chips. The color of your car, of course, is the last one sprayed on. A paint chip from a vehicle will have a layer of primer coat, sealant, paint, and perhaps even a lacquer finish.

A prime example in which paint chips are commonly examined as evidence is in crime scenes of negligent homicides, where vehicles have crashed together or even when a vehicle hit a pedestrian and fled. In such cases, the Locard Theory screams out, "See, I told you!"

Cigarettes and Tobacco

"But cigarettes are not really small items," you say. Yet cigarettes and cigarette butts are considered trace evidence.

There was a young man who liked to watch things blow up. He didn't want to hurt anyone, but he really enjoyed watching the explosions. So he took his hobby to open fields in Mānoa, usually school playgrounds or the district park, where he would explode his home-made bombs.

Because he didn't want to hurt anyone, he exploded his bombs at night. Nighttime also offered him a better opportunity to watch the explosion. His modus operandi (Latin for method of operation), also known as an MO, was that he would walk about the open field, making sure no one else was present. He didn't want to accidentally hurt anyone and he certainly didn't want to get caught. He then would select a location to explode his bomb, walk a distance away, and sit down. Our polite bomber would then patiently watch to ensure he was completely alone. When he felt completely safe, he would walk back to his site, place the bomb, light the fuse, and run quickly to his safe spot and watch the bomb explode. The bomb would go off, scaring the neighborhood, and our polite bomber would get his jollies.

But while he watched and waited to ensure he was alone, he would smoke. At each scene where he set off bombs, he would smoke. And he chain-smoked—the same brand at each site. Some cigarettes he would smoke to the butt. Some he would smoke only halfway. We learned several things from his nasty smoking habit. We determined his MO regarding his sitting and waiting. This enabled us to recover very small samples of saliva (which was enough for later ABO blood-typing comparison, which we'll discuss further in the following chapter), and we obtained fingerprints. We eventually caught the young man, who pleaded that he didn't hurt anyone, that his passion was harmless. "Come on, give me a break!" he insisted. I think some of the officers wanted to break a few of his bones.

Some people who smoke cigarettes and cigars and who chew tobacco tend to leave a lot of saliva behind—cigar smokers and tobacco chewers in particular. Have you ever watched a person who chews tobacco? He has to spit every few seconds. And the polite ones spit into an empty soda can. If he leaves that can behind and happens to be a suspect in a crime, it's a treasure to the crime scene technician—not a very clean one, but a treasure nonetheless. The saliva can be tested and later compared to the suspect's blood type. If it didn't help us catch criminals, this might be yet another reason not to have anything to do with tobacco.

There's a story of how these things can go too far, however. We had an old and stubborn detective tell a young and intelligent crime scene technician to pick up *all* the cigarette butts at a baseball field where the body of a man was found beaten to death. There must have been 150 or more cigarette butts. The technician objected mildly.

"You really want only those relatively fresh cigarette butts, right?"

"No," he said. "Every one."

"But the body is fresh," the technician complained. "Some of these butts are weeks old."

"I'm the detective," he said. "You're the lowly technician. Do as you're told."

It was at this point that I looked up "old-time detectives" in the police dictionary and found that they are synonymous with the word "dinosaurs." We intervened, and intelligence replaced the rut that was deeply engraved in that detective's brain. He must have watched too many TV police dramas.

Matches

Matches can be left at crime scenes by suspects who smoke or by just plain dumb crooks who use them as "flashlights." The primary good of this evidence is learning the suspect's MO. If he does this in one case, odds are he'll do this in other cases. Comparison of the match with the stub is another possibility, if you're lucky enough to catch the crook with the book of matches in his pocket—the same book from which he tore off and lit matches at the crime scene. Some crooks also like to chew on matches. (If you're a crook and reading this book, please don't chew on the lit end of the match.) The match then becomes a good source of saliva to test for ABO blood typing.

In the 1970s, when I was a motor-patrol officer in Kāneʻohe, I participated in the arrest of a not-too-smart crook who lit matches when he burglarized homes at night. Later in the 1980s, as a detective, I worked on a series of cases in Kāhala where some homes were burglarized at night by a crook who left burnt matches at the crime scenes. I remembered the guy from the 1970s but didn't have enough evidence to accuse him. So with my partner, I drove to his home, knocked on his door, and when he answered, merely pulled a book of matches from my shirt pocket, held it out to him, and said, "Remember me?" The poor man hung his head and immediately confessed. Sometimes you really need luck. It also helps to have a dumb crook as well.

Glass

There's broken glass everywhere—not necessarily the large shards that result when you drop a water glass, but the tiny, ground-down particles that you can barely see. (Many states add ground glass to road asphalt.) In cases where a scuffle results in broken glass, we can check the suspect's shoes or even feet for trace glass that we can compare to the glass at the scene.

Today, the safety glass used for automobile windshields and other materials has a plastic laminate to prevent shattering. But if you can find a piece of glass that is not manufactured as safety glass, it may have some interesting characteristics that could be very important to CSIs.

When a bullet passes through nonsafety glass, you may see a fracture pattern that looks like a spider web. Two types of fractures occur here: concentric fractures and radial fractures. The diagram below shows a single bullet passing through the glass.

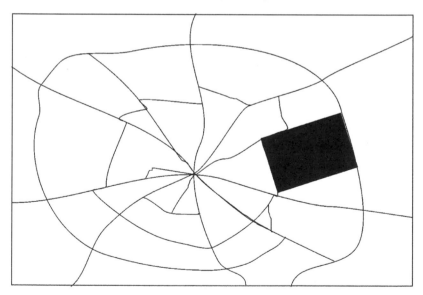

It is possible—albeit not likely because the glass would probably shatter—that you can tell which bullet was fired first in such fractures if a second shot was fired. The identical spider-weblike fractures will occur again, but will be confined to that area inside preexisting fractures, as shown below.

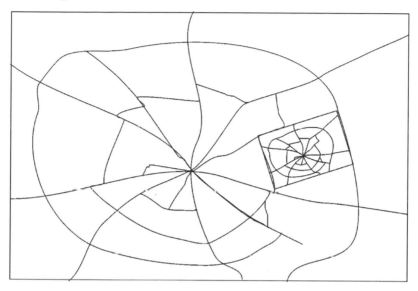

The first shot created the larger spider-weblike pattern. The second shot created the spider-weblike pattern inside a smaller pane bordered by fractures.

It is also possible to tell in which direction the bullet was traveling when the shot was fired. When a bullet strikes a pane of glass, it will form a crater with the large opening of the crater on the side opposite that which was struck first by the bullet, as shown in the diagram below.

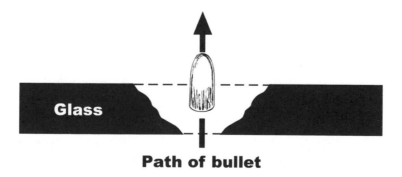

When a crook breaks a pane of glass to gain entry and the cops catch that guy, it is important to examine the crook's clothing for glass splinters or tiny particles of glass. When struck, the shattering glass will cause some particles to fly backward toward the suspect.

Glass can be examined for many things: color, density, thickness, refractive index, and chemical composition. These characteristics help distinguish one pane of glass from another. Therefore it's important to understand that *all that glitters is not from the same broken pane of glass.*

Soil and Vegetation

Dirt can be an important item of trace evidence. Soil is much more than mere dirt. I wash mere dirt off my two young children every night during their bath—which can be a very trying experience, especially since at their tender age they seem to think they need a bath only once a year.

Soil, on the other hand, contains all kinds of information. Look at footwear, at tires, and at feet if you can. You'll find minerals, small pieces of plant material, and tiny rocks. Soil can be analyzed chemically and for comparison.

In Hawai'i, the native soil comes from one common source: that maternal hot spot that spewed all the lava to form the various islands. But over the ages, soil from different parts of each island has developed its own characteristics. Just look at the red dirt from Mililani in contrast to the usually sandy soil of Kailua. The Mililani soil is likely to have many more chemicals in it than Kailua's (even though the developers tell you it doesn't). This is because the soil has been used for farming, and farmers introduce chemicals to kill the insects that eat the plants. The Mililani land was used in large part for growing sugarcane and pineapple. That soil has a high concentration of chemicals. Let's take the example of a killing that occurred in Kailua, after which the suspects took the body to Mililani to dump it. If they drove and walked through the red dirt of one of those old sugarcane and pineapple fields, it is quite probable that some of that dirt was transferred to the tires of their car, their shoes and clothing, and then onto the floor of the car. The trick is to find the car, which would most likely have good circumstantial evidence that it was in Mililani's red dirt.

Plant material is also readily transferable from shoes to vehicle and from ground to tire and underside of vehicle. Three drug dealers who lived on the Leeward coast took a fourth man (who unfortunately didn't pay his drug bills) to Waimānalo. They drove off the road through tall brush, pulled the victim out of the car, and shot him in the head. His body was found and samples of the vegetation were recovered for possible future use. What's nice about drug-related killings is that people high on drugs talk. It didn't take long before the dead guy's friends were telling us who killed him. After a little more interrogation, one of the people involved in the killing pointed his finger at the actual shooter. We found the car, got a search warrant, and recovered vegetation from under the vehicle. It was the same type of vegetation found in the field they drove through. This was not enough evidence to directly prove a fact but enough to argue in court that it corroborated the statement of the witness who ratted out his friends.

So remember, clean and scrub down your kids, at least once a week, before they're recovered as circumstantial evidence.

Wood

Wood as trace evidence does not refer to a tree. A tree, of course, was its ancestor, and that piece of wooden evidence is now in a different form. While many aspects of wood can be considered for forensic analysis—such as hardness or softness, age, and axe or saw cuts—some of the more spectacular forensic applications have come from tiny splinters.

In 1988 twenty-four-year-old Marialyse Catell was murdered by her husband, Michael. This case is described in detail in *Honolulu Homicide*. Michael Catell was seen dragging a wooden footlocker that contained his wife's body. When we processed the scene, we recovered a tiny sliver of wood. A few days later, the footlocker was found at a downtown pier. Through close examination, we were able to fit that splinter exactly into the tiny groove of wood it had come from. It was a valuable link from the crime scene to the suspect.

Hair

Hair is something I'm losing at an extraordinary rate. Actually, we all are. Put a clean white pillowcase on your pillow. Go to sleep. When you wake up, look at the pillowcase. You should see from a few to many hairs on the clean linen. We all lose hair.

Now think about a violent crime in which there was physical contact between suspect and victim. We can probably expect that there will be hair transfer. In fights, hair may even be pulled out of a person's head.

If the evidence is determined to be hair—because remember, it could be a fiber—the first thing we do need to know is if it is human or not. If you own a pet, look around. You'll probably see your pet's hair, assuming it's not a fish, a reptile, or a bird. Once we determine it is human, it can be examined for important characteristics.

First, human hair is diverse in its characteristics. Head hair is normally pretty uniform, but sometimes the hair at the back of your head is a little thicker than that up front. Beard hair is curved and coarse. Hair from the chest and back tends to be finer and, under the microscope, tends to have graduated tips. Pubic hair is wiry and has uneven pigmentation. Using a microscope, we can examine pigmentation. We cut the hair in a cross-section and examine shape characteristics. These help us to make a determination of racial origin.

We can even determine the gender of the person who lost the hair through examination of follicular cells, whereby a scientist can determine the X-Y chromosome score. We cannot tell age. We cannot tell height or weight. Inevitably, I catch a few forensic students on a hair exam question by stating that age is easily determined through hair examination.

A most important characteristic about hair is that it has roots.

And if that root is intact (and you have enough hair), you might be able to conduct a DNA analysis. Depending on the circumstances surrounding the case, this fact could be extremely important. Take the example of a rape victim who, in the course of her struggle with her attacker, pulls out some hair with roots attached. If a suspect is subsequently identified, a DNA analysis and comparison can be conducted and potential identification may be obtained.

Fibers

Fiber evidence is as important as hair evidence. We shed fibers—perhaps not as quickly as we shed hair—and fiber evidence can be found at almost every crime where there has been violent physical contact.

Generally, fibers will fall into one of four broad categories that are very similar to those in the child's guessing game played on long car trips: animal, mineral, vegetable, and (in the case of fibers) synthetic.

Natural animal hair is classified as hair unless it is specifically used as a fiber in the manufacture of clothing. Examples of these are wool, camel's hair, and—particularly inappropriate these days—fur.

Vegetable fibers are also associated with clothing made of cotton and linen, as well as with ropes made of hemp and jute.

Fibers considered to be mineral are asbestos, glass wool, and fiberglass, even though they may be manmade. The key is that there is an association with minerals as a characteristic.

Finally, synthetic fibers that don't fall into the mineral category can also be associated with clothing, such as rayon, nylon, and polyesters.

As with hair, fibers are examined through the microscope. In making these examinations, we look for characteristics and features such as the following:
- color
- surface appearance
- cross-sectional shape

- diameter
- fluorescence

A Final Word

The interesting thing about wood, hair, fibers, or any other type of trace evidence is that investigators just don't know exactly what they're looking for until they find it. It's there hiding. Edmund Locard proved that. Once the evidence is found, it becomes the job of all the police investigators and crime scene technicians around the world to decide exactly what to do with it.

Trace Evidence Experiment #1: Evidence on the Bottom of Your Shoes

Equipment:
1. Your work shoes
2. Debris-free, stiff brush
3. Sheet of clean white paper

Gather your work shoes and take them to a work surface. With a clean, debris-free brush with stiff bristles, slowly brush the soles of your shoes, allowing any objects or particles from the soles to fall onto the clean white sheet of paper.

After you've brushed the soles of both shoes, carefully examine the paper. It is quite possible that you will find tiny glass particles, fibers, hair, soil, and plant material (in addition to the gum you stepped on yesterday on the sidewalk).

If you get nothing, where you walking for your shoes to be so damn clean?

Trace Evidence Experiment #2: Hair Samples

Equipment:
1. Pair of tweezers
2. Magnifying glass
3. Several small squares of clean white paper

Set up the squares of paper in front of you. Using the tweezers, pluck a few strands of hair from your head, then from your chest (assuming you are male), then from your arms, and then from your legs. Go someplace private and yank a few pubic hairs as well.

Using the magnifying glass, look at each hair, making notes on the paper squares of the hair's color, texture (fine, medium, coarse), and other shape characteristics. You should be able to see different characteristics among the different hairs from different locations on your body.

If all your hair is similar, either you were too embarrassed to pull hairs from different places on your body, or you and I are going to make a ton of money in a side show.

Trace Evidence Experiment #3: Fibers

This chapter gave several examples of the different types of fibers in each of the four broad categories. Your task: Identify at least two of the more common examples in each category.

Animal:

1._____

2._____

Vegetable:

1._____

2._____

Mineral:

1._____

2._____

Synthetic:

1._____

2._____

Trace Evidence Experiment #4: The Clean Shirt
Equipment:
1. Clean, just washed and dried T-shirt (color does not matter, but white works well)
2. Manual, nonelectric timer
3. Magnifying glass
4. Pair of tweezers
5. Volunteer (preferably your honey)

Check out the T-shirt and remove any objects—hair, fibers, lint from the dryer—anything you can find stuck to the shirt. Put the shirt on.

Set the timer to one minute. Start the timer. Wrestle with your honey on top of your rug for exactly one minute. Be careful so that nobody gets hurt. If you don't have a rug, wrestle on the floor—just be more careful.

After one minute, stop. I said stop! Any further activity can wait for later in the evening. Take off your T-shirt. Examine it with the magnifying glass. Use the tweezers to remove all the items that have collected on your T-shirt.

Unbelievable, huh? There should be a large number of things attached to your T-shirt. Fibers from the rug, hair—yours and your honey's—and a whole lot of other things. If nothing is there, tell whoever cleaned your rug to come my house. I can use the help.

You are now free to turn your attention back to your honey.

4
Blood

I once knew a detective, Joe Thursday, who desperately wanted to become a homicide detective. On a quiet Saturday morning, Thursday got his chance. I was called at home by the Criminal Investigation Division (CID) weekend lieutenant and notified that there was a killing at a Wai'anae apartment. A man had stabbed his girlfriend to death.

Detective Thursday had already been sent to the scene to begin preliminary investigation. I notified the team of detectives waiting for the next murder investigation assignment and drove out to the scene. When I got there, I met with the patrol officer standing "sentry duty" outside the apartment to prevent any additional unauthorized persons from entering the scene. I asked him where Detective Thursday was. The officer pointed to the building's parking lot and said, "He's sitting in his car."

I walked over to the detective's car and found him sitting in the passenger seat with the backrest set in a reclining position. He was holding his forehead and looked as pale as a white sheet of paper.

"You okay?" I remember asking. He tried to speak, but each time his words would get caught in his throat and he looked as if he would hurl his breakfast.

"Have you been inside the scene?" He nodded affirmatively.

"The CID lieutenant says witnesses saw the victim's boyfriend running from the apartment. Anything on him?" He nodded yes again and bumped his wrists together, indicating that the man had been arrested and handcuffed.

"Come see me when you feel a little better," I instructed. Again he nodded.

I walked back to the apartment. The officer standing guard said that the victim was in the bathroom. I carefully walked in, looking at a few drops of blood on the living room carpet, making sure I didn't step on any of them. The woman was lying on her side in the bathroom, propped up against a wall. The walls were painted a bright white, but I would guess that 90 percent of those white walls were covered with blood spatter. Looking around the room, I could see, in addition to the blood spatter on the walls, a lot of blood staining the sink and the countertop. The water in the toilet was a deep red. The toilet seat was dripping with blood. The bathtub was also stained red. Running down the center of the floor of the tub was a red discoloration where the blood had flowed down the tub and into the drain.

The woman was dressed in a light-colored slip or nightgown, but that, too, was almost completely covered in blood. I could see that she had deep lacerations and puncture wounds to her hands. There was a tear in her arm. A portion of her neck was torn open. There were many small tears in her slip, telling me where the knife tore through her garment and into her chest and stomach. None of her wounds were bleeding. It appeared that her tongue was sticking out of her mouth, but upon closer examination, I saw it was red foam oozing from her throat. The smell of blood as it began to decay was very strong.

The officer interrupted at that point. "Lieutenant, Detective Thursday is here to see you."

Thursday was standing just outside the door. He was still pale and looked ill, but he was able to speak. He quickly admitted that he never realized a stabbing could be so brutal, that there could be so much blood, or that the wounds could be so horrible. And the smell—he could smell it even standing outside the house.

Blood putrefies quickly, so it must be handled very carefully. As it decays, it exudes a peculiarly sweet smell that most people don't forget. And the sight of blood, especially a lot of blood, can be sickening to some people. I completely understood what had overcome

Detective Thursday, and I remember feeling compassion for his reaction to the sight of that murdered woman. And we never heard about his wanting to become a detective in the Homicide Detail again.

Understanding blood and the various analyses that can be conducted are critically important to the investigation of a violent crime, and every effort must be given to the proper identification and recovery of blood samples and to their laboratory analysis. Further, the crime scene investigator must understand the capabilities of laboratory analyses in order to request the examinations needed in each case.

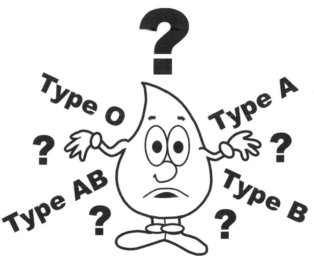

Blood Types

Do you know your blood type? If not, why not? All of us should, at some point in our life, find out what our blood type is. You can never tell when it will become important—in an emergency room, in a vampire's office, at a crime scene.

There are four blood types: A, B, AB, and O. I once gave an exam asking students to write down the different blood types. One student wrote down A, B, AB, and C—an indication of his grade to come. (Actually, my exams are fairly easy if my students study their lecture notes.)

When we ask for a determination of blood type, the lab test we're asking for is known as ABO typing. ABO typing is nice to know, but if there is only a small amount of blood to analyze, we don't waste it on ABO typing. About 80 percent of all people are combined Type A or Type O blood types. The ABO typing analysis does not prove anything except the blood type of the sample. I personally prefer to save a small sample for DNA analysis.

Secretors

Like Type A and Type O people, about 80 percent of the population are secretors. This word conjures up all kinds of thoughts: people with drooling problems, people who ooze something through their pores—yuck!

Actually, you're probably a secretor yourself. Secretors are people who have ABO grouping substances in most of their bodily fluids—saliva, semen, and vaginal fluid, for example. By examining such fluids, we may be able to determine blood type. Again, it's nice to have, but not as critical as novelists tend to suggest.

DNA

Thank you, God, for acronyms, because it would be very cumbersome to say deoxyribonucleic acid each time I needed to. Go ahead, try it again: deoxyribonucleic acid. Perhaps after a while, you'll even come to learn how to spell it without looking.

DNA is a biological condition of our body's chemical composition that makes us different from one another. You probably have seen a representation of DNA in the form of a double helix, which looks like a ladder that has been twisted. The steps of this ladder, or double helix, are bases of chemical information known as guanine, adenine, thymine, and cytosine.

Okay, wake up—enough science. All you

The double helix

need to know is that DNA analysis is pretty good at identifying or eliminating people as suspects in criminal cases.

There is a problem with DNA analysis, however. It has to do with the population data banks used by labs that do the analyses. Each data bank is supposed to represent an average cross-section of the community from which it was taken. For example, if the data bank in Alabama is composed of a majority of samples taken from white, black, and Hispanic people, it could probably be argued by an attorney that the data bank was unfair in its representation because his client had a mixture of Chinese and Hawaiian ancestry.

This could create a big problem in Hawai'i. The DNA data banks need samples that come from "pure" races or ethnicities: pure Chinese, pure Japanese, pure Caucasian, pure black—and pure Hawaiian. Are there any pure Hawaiians left? Of course, but their numbers are very small. What could be an even bigger problem is that there are numerous people with "mixed" blood. Such a database would have to collect several hundred samples from each "mixture" in order to obtain a fair representation of our population. This is literally an impossible task. When I ask about ethnic background in my classes, I get a wide range of answers, but the winner has got to be a young woman from the University of Hawai'i–West O'ahu, who said she was Hawaiian, Chinese, Puerto Rican, Vietnamese, English, French, and Dutch, and she thought she might have a little bit of Portuguese on her mother's side. Personally, I think her last claim was for my benefit.

Perhaps the world of science will end up using averages, because it will be extraordinarily difficult to obtain a database of several hundred people who have the racial mix of Hawaiian, Chinese, Puerto Rican, Vietnamese, English, French, Dutch, and a little bit of Portuguese.

Presumptive Tests for Missing Blood Stains

"Hey, sweetheart, is that blood on the koa mantelpiece, or the remnant stain of some gecko poop?" There are many really good homicide detectives and crime scene investigators—but not *that* good. None of these great crime scene detectives can tell whether blood has been cleaned up from a crime scene—that is, not without help.

Oftentimes crime scenes are processed long after the crime occurred. The Diane Suzuki case described in *Honolulu Homicide* is an example of that. I attended a murder seminar where one presenter described an Oregon homicide in which a man was reported missing. The detective, for reasons only his psyche could tell, suspected the man's grieving wife. Twenty years went by and the case remained open. Then one day, the use of the chemical luminol was introduced in police investigations. The detective, now contemplating retirement, used this new technology to obtain a search warrant (in the same way we obtained a search warrant in the Suzuki case, five years after she disappeared). That detective removed the rug from the living room in the woman's house, conducted the luminol test, and discovered that a large pool of blood had been cleaned up some time before. Confronted with that information, the woman confessed and took the detective to a location in the woods behind her house where she had buried her husband after shooting him in the head—twenty years earlier.

Luminol

Luminol was invented in 1973 by Walter Sprecht, and it was gradually adopted as a useful tool for crime scene investigators. Its emergence in Hawai'i in the 1980s has been a tremendous help. Now its use is commonplace, and it's as if it has always existed.

First of all, don't believe the TV shows that show you luminol glowing like the sun during the daylight hours. Luminol is luminescent, which means it will give off a faint glow in the dark. And that dark needs to be almost total. Light infiltrating a room will interfere with the luminescing process, and investigators could miss a positive result. Luminol works best on old bloodstains, and it can produce good results long after the blood has been cleaned. On the negative side, it reacts with metal, producing the same blue glow. Caution must be used to ensure that luminol is not glowing because of its contact with a metal surface.

Applying luminol is not that difficult. If the investigators suspect an area has been cleaned of blood spilled during a crime, the room must be darkened as much as possible. The luminol reagent is sprayed lightly via an aerosol sprayer. If blood has been there in the past, it will briefly glow blue. Then investigators turn on the lights and set up a camera over the area that glowed. With the lights on, they take a picture of the area but they do not advance the frame. Then they turn off the lights and spray again, this time spraying a little every few seconds. As the area brightens and glows, they open the camera's iris and allow it to remain open for about two minutes. The glow of the reaction will burn into the picture taken with the light on. When the picture is processed, the investigators should have a photo that shows the lighted area—and the glowing blue reaction.

Please do not attempt to try this yourself if you have access to luminol. The health hazards of the chemical are not completely known, and it has been suggested by some that it is carcinogenic.

Phenolphthalin

Phenolphthalin is another commonly used presumptive test for blood. This test, unlike luminol, is used on visible blood as well as in locations where blood is suspected to have been. The use of phenolphthalin is simple. Investigators need cotton swabs, a saline solution, and phenolphthalin. When a drop that could be blood or gecko poop is found, they take a cotton swab, put a few drops of saline solution on its tip to moisten it, rub it lightly on the stain, and finally add one drop of phenolphthalin to the swab. If the stain is blood, the tip will instantly turn purple. If it does not turn purple instantaneously, it's not blood. But note that phenolphthalin will eventually turn purple, so negative swabs should be placed immediately in a bag marked "negative swabs" to prevent confusion.

In areas where investigators suspect that blood has been cleaned up, they can still use the phenolphthalin and luminol tests.

A double-positive reaction is powerful circumstantial evidence. With any chemical, all care and caution should be observed.

Bloodstain Pattern Analysis

It is highly likely that blood will be spilled at violent crime scenes. Blood can come from gunshot wounds, knife wounds, blunt trauma wounds (the result of hitting someone with a baseball bat or similar weapon), and a variety of other means.

When blood strikes a surface, it's called blood spatter. This spatter forms a pattern that can be examined through a process known as bloodstain pattern analysis.

The shape of blood spatter depends on a variety of things: the height from which blood fell, the angle at which it struck the surface, the force and speed with which the blood was expelled from the wound, and the quantity of blood in each blood drop.

A note of caution is appropriate here. It is widely known that blood can present a biological hazard and the risk of contracting hepatitis and AIDS. Any crime scene investigator dealing with blood should take precautions to prevent contact: wear eye protection, surgical gloves, a surgical mask, and footwear protection such as surgical booties.

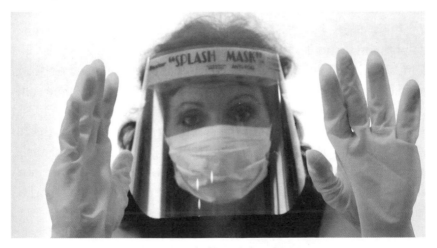

Protective clothing and equipment

The shape of the blood drop may be used to determine the angle and direction from which it struck the surface. However, the characteristic of the surface will also have an effect on the shape of the blood drop; for example, the shape of the blood drop will change if the surface is smooth or pebbly.

The distance that the drop fell is also a factor in the shape of the drop. The characteristics of the rim, or edge, of the blood drop come into play primarily with blood drops that have fallen at a 90-degree angle (straight down). A blood drop falling at 90 degrees from a height of up to about twenty inches will look perfectly round. From a height between about twenty to forty inches, it will have large scallops along its rim; from between about forty to sixty inches, it will have scallops that are fine and pointy; from between about sixty to eighty inches, it will have fine pointy scallops that burst out like flares on the surface of the sun. From a height of more than eighty inches, the blood drop may burst and spatter outward.

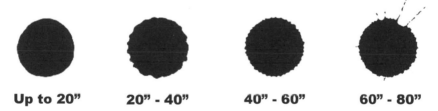

Up to 20"   **20" - 40"**   **40" - 60"**   **60" - 80"**

Blood drops hitting a surface from left to right at an increasingly greater height.

A blood drop falling at other than a right angle will result in a teardrop shape. The elongation of the drop will depend on the angle with which the drop strikes the surface. One unique characteristic is that the pointed ends of the teardrop indicate the direction of flight. The greater the angle, the greater the possibility that the drop itself will appear long and narrow and will throw off smaller teardrop spatter known as cast-off patterns.

Blood is a liquid that is uniform and has a greater viscosity than water. It will produce the same patterns in different cases, and those patterns will not be affected by temperature or humidity.

Training and experience in CSIs where blood has been spilled will help the investigators reconstruct the events surrounding the manner and occurrence of the blood spatter by using bloodstain pattern analysis. This is shown in our discussion of the Roland Kotani murder in *Honolulu Homicide*.

High-Velocity Blood Spatter

When a person is wounded with a gun or some other high-velocity weapon, an effect called high-velocity blood spatter will often occur. This happens because of the high-speed impact and the resulting pressure associated with that impact.

Unlike the blood-drop type of blood spatter discussed above, high-velocity blood spatter looks like the saliva exiting a person's mouth during a sneeze or cough.

Arterial Blood Spatter

Arterial blood spatter can be identified by the large quantity or clumps of blood thrown off from a wound onto a surface. If that surface is a wall, the clump of blood will usually be accompanied by a trail of blood that descends from the clump toward the floor or ground.

Other Blood Examinations

Investigations involving the examination and analysis of blood are not limited to ABO typing, DNA, or bloodstain pattern analysis. There are other serological examinations that investigators can turn to depending on the circumstances of the case.

Human or Not

Whether or not blood collected from a crime scene is human can be determined through laboratory testing. This could be important when a suspect claims that the blood found outside his home is that of an injured animal or when an injured victim claims he was beaten by a suspect.

Sexing

Sexing simply means that it is possible, through blood evidence examination, to determine the gender of the person from whom the blood came. If a suspect is injured, this could be yet another piece of the evidence puzzle needed to convict.

Race

In some cases, it may be possible to determine the race of the person from whom the blood came. Laboratory analysis seems to show that hemoglobin types can be ethnic specific and thus imply the race of the person whose blood was recovered from the crime scene.

Blood of Menstrual Origin

There may be a need to determine whether blood collected off the skin of a rape suspect is menstrual in origin. It could serve as important evidence if a woman rape victim identifies the suspect as her attacker. Combine this with a positive DNA analysis that the blood matches the victim, and there is tremendous evidence that the suspect is the assailant.

Feces Examination

In sodomy assaults, it may be possible to obtain a feces sample from the suspect. It is possible to differentiate between human and animal feces, and microscopic examination of the feces may show similarities in undigested foods, which with a positive comparison from the victim may become strong circumstantial evidence that the suspect is the assailant.

Urine Examination

Urine is another body fluid that can sometimes be part of a sexual assault. Further tests on urine and blood type can produce positive results that can substantiate a victim's statement accusing a particular suspect.

A Final Word

As Shakespeare wrote in *The Merchant of Venice,* "If you prick us, do we not bleed?"

Yes, we do. And when that blood is left at a crime scene, it can tell us many things about what happened and about who was involved. If the crime scene is a murder, the blood can tell us a story.

But John Webster suggested in *The Duchess of Malfi* that in murder cases, that bloody crime scene does more than just tell us a story. He wrote, "Other sins only speak; murder shrieks out."

Blood Experiment #1: Blood Spatter Recognition, Part 1: Blood-Drop Angle Analysis

Equipment:

1. One cup of water
2. Light Karo syrup
3. Red food coloring
4. Sheet of plain white paper
5. Clipboard or sheet of cardboard to which the paper can be attached
6. Eyedropper

7. Compass

Put the cup of water into a mixing bowl. Slowly add a tablespoon of Karo syrup at a time until the liquid has the texture of maple syrup or pancake syrup—a liquid thicker than water, but not as thick and slow as honey. When you feel you have a liquid that has about the viscosity of blood, add a few drops of red food coloring for effect.

Attach the paper to the clipboard or cardboard. Lay the paper flat on the floor, take some of the red liquid into the eyedropper, and allow a drop to fall at 90 degrees to the paper from a height of twenty inches. Repeat at forty, sixty, and eighty inches to observe the effect of height in a 90-degree blood spatter.

With the assistance of a partner, let a drop fall while holding the paper at different angles (use a compass) to observe the effect of angles on a falling blood drop.

If this doesn't work, I don't know what to say. Go back and make your "blood" thicker and try again.

Blood Experiment #2: Blood Spatter Recognition, Part 2: Bloodstain Pattern Analysis

Equipment:

1. Two tablespoons of the Karo-water mixture from Experiment #1
2. Clean kitchen sponge
3. Sheet of plain white paper
4. Clipboard or sheet of cardboard to which the paper can be attached

Clip, glue, or staple the paper to the clipboard or cardboard. Set it up on a kitchen counter so it is standing at a 90-degree angle to the countertop. Put the two tablespoons of the Karo-water mixture onto the sponge. Set the sponge down on the counter about two feet away from the paper. Make a fist. Slam your fist into the sponge. Observe the pattern the liquid mixture makes on the paper—kitchen counter, walls, floor, ceiling, windows, and curtains!

Stay away from your spouse or parents for a few hours and deny the existence of this experiment. Practice the phrase, "I don't know what you're talking about."

Blood Experiment #3: Blood Spatter Recognition, Part 3: Bloodstain Pattern Analysis

Equipment needed:

1. Two tablespoons of the Karo-water mixture from Experiment #1
2. Sheet of plain white paper
3. Clipboard or sheet of cardboard to which the paper can be attached

Affix the paper to the clipboard or cardboard. Take two tablespoons of the liquid and place it into your mouth. Don't swallow. Stand in the kitchen. Hold the paper at arm's length, perpendicular to the floor. Inhale deeply through your nose. Purse your lips and blow out really hard, imitating a long, loud, and explosive sneeze. Observe that the high-velocity "bloodstain" pattern is now on the paper—kitchen counter, walls, floor, ceiling, windows, and curtains!

Stay away from your spouse or parents for a few hours and again deny the existence of this experiment—or even this book.

5
Firearms

The first thing we need to know about a firearm is whether it's a gun or not—that is, in the strictest terms of the law. If someone is to be charged for certain firearm offenses, such as no permit to carry a firearm, the gun must work. In other cases, such as robbery, using a gun that has had molten lead poured down its barrel to make it inoperable is not the issue because the crook is using the gun to frighten the victim. In most offenses where a firearm has been involved, it's important to ensure that the gun works, so it needs to be examined and test-fired.

Firearm Characteristics

All firearms are made up of similar parts: the body or frame of the weapon; a means of holding ammunition and sending it to the next firing position; a firing pin; a handle or stock of some kind; and a barrel. It's the barrel that can be the most important part.

The *barrel* is a hollow cylinder made from one piece of metal to keep it from bursting at the seams upon firing. The *bore* of the barrel is the hollow "tube" that travels from one end to the other. Bores can be rifled or not. *Rifling* means that there are grooves cut into the barrel. These grooves make about a quarter turn from one end to the other, like a twist of licorice or a barber's pole. This turn causes the bullet to spin as it exits the bore. The twist of the grooves helps to keep the bullet flying straight and true, rather than flying wildly once it leaves the barrel. The groove portion of the rifling is called—ready?—the *groove*. The raised portion is called the *land*. The rifling can be a right- or a left-hand rifling, depending on the manufacturer. Shotguns, however, do not have any rifling. That's because with a shotgun, which is supposed to be used for hunting or police purposes, the shotgun pellets are intended to spread into a burst pattern as they escape the bore. This spread gives the pellets a better opportunity to strike the target.

The *caliber* is usually thought of by most people as the size of the bullet. This is not so. Caliber is the distance between two opposite lands in the bore, usually measured in millimeters, and this distance is an approximation; it's not quite perfect. Therefore, when we say a bullet is a .38 caliber bullet, we're actually referring to the weapon's bore measurement. We won't be able to change this common misconception, but at least now *you* know the correct definition. Shotguns, of course, have to be different. A shotgun's bore is measured by its *gauge*. And, even more confusing, the diameter of the bore increases as the number of the gauge gets smaller. Therefore, the diameter of the bore of a 20-gauge shotgun is smaller than the diameter of the bore of a 12-gauge shotgun.

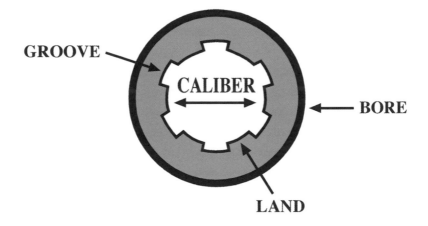

Classes of Firearms

There are two classes of firearms: shoulder weapons, such as rifles and shotguns, and handguns, such as revolvers and pistols.

Shoulder Weapons
Shoulder weapons usually have long bores and the capability of

firing larger and more powerful bullets than handguns. The term *shoulder* means that usually, because of the weight of the weapon, shooters need to brace the weapon with their shoulder in order to get a more accurate aim and to maintain control of the weapon after it has been fired. The "kick" of some of these shoulder firearms can be pretty strong. It's not uncommon for police recruits learning to fire shotguns and rifles to come away with bruises on their shoulders and cuts to their lips and foreheads when they don't control their rifles or shotguns properly.

Double-barreled shotguns have barrels side by side and can shoot one or two shells with one pull of the trigger. Most shotguns require you to "pump" the slide to remove the spent shell and insert a new one. Double-barreled shotguns "break" just after the firing pin. The barrel folds down, allowing the removal of the spent shells by hand and the insertion of the new ones. These guns are made primarily for hunting because a hunter can shoot double the amount of shot at the same time.

Handguns

The term *handgun* is self-explanatory: a gun that can be held in and fired by the hand. This category includes all types of handguns, from revolvers to semiautomatic pistols or even to weapons such as derringers, designed to shoot either a single shot or two shots, like the double-barreled shotgun. This type of derringer, however, has its barrels one on top of the other, sometimes called over-and-under.

Revolvers are handguns that hold the bullets in a cylinder that rotates when each shot is fired, moving another bullet into position for the next shot. Semiautomatic guns operate on the gas that occurs when the gunpowder in the bullet explodes. The gas helps to force the used bullet out, and a spring in the bullet clip moves the next bullet into position. Semiautomatic guns are called pistols to differentiate them from revolvers. Semiautomatic guns have become preferable to revolvers because they can hold more bullets.

Ammunition

Up to this point, I've referred to ammunition as bullets. That's not entirely correct. A bullet is only the front portion of what is correctly termed a "cartridge." The cartridge is made up of several things: the lead projectile, correctly called a bullet, the shell casing, gunpowder, and a primer.

The Bullet

Bullets are generally made of a lead alloy, commonly shaped into a curving cone. About half of the bullet is hidden in the cartridge, where it is snugly held in place by the shell casing. Bullets can also be covered with a harder metal—sometimes brass, sometimes copper. If so, the bullet is said to be "jacketed." It can be semijacketed or fully jacketed. The intent behind jacketing a bullet is to keep it as intact as possible when it strikes an object. Normally when a lead bullet strikes an object, it flattens or even breaks apart. The full jacket helps to reduce this, but semijacketed bullets "blossom" like a flower, which means that they usually do more damage to whomever or whatever they hit.

The Shell Casing and Gunpowder

The shell casing is a harder metal than the bullet and is hollow to hold the gunpowder. Gunpowder is not true powder; rather, it's tiny pellets or discs of nitrocellulose in a powder base or black powder. When this material is confined in a shell casing and ignited, it burns very rapidly. It does not explode.

"But what about that explosion I hear?" you ask.

It's the sound of the pressure causing the bullet to rapidly break free of the shell casing. The powder truly burns, giving off a very great quantity of gas for its size. It's that expanding gas that propels the bullet out of the barrel and from the gun.

Various members of the Scientific Investigation Section and I were at an exposition at the Bishop Museum. We had a booth that included a variety of firearm-related items. One of our staff members was demonstrating to a group of grade-school kids that gunpowder truly burns and does not explode. He had several trays of different types of gunpowder and, using long fireplace matches, he would light the powder in each tray. The burning powder ignited rapidly with a loud *whoosh* and puffs of smoke. One tray was stubborn. The tech kept trying to ignite it and it wouldn't burn—until he leaned over it. The *whoosh* and brief burst of flame left him with curly eyebrows and a little less hair on the front of his head. The kids burst into laughter, and some shouted, "Do it again!"

The Primer

Each cartridge has a primer—pronounced like the paint primer you apply before the final color—at its base. The primer is a highly volatile charge that is shock sensitive, and when it is ignited it further ignites the powder in the casing. There are two types of primer: rimfire and centerfire. These names define where the primer is located on the base of the shell casing; for some it's just on the rim, and with others it's in the center. Almost all .22 caliber ammunition is rimfire. The primer is the only part of a cartridge that explodes. It's made up of a different material than the powder and so it gives off a different residue than gunpowder. It is examination of this residue that can help police determine whether a person fired a gun.

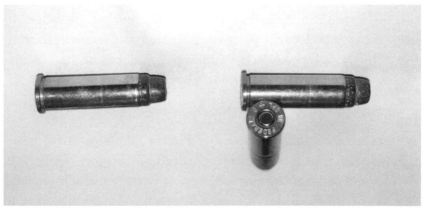

The characteristics of an ammunition cartridge

Evidence from Firearm Examination

There are various things that can be done with firearm evidence outside of processing the weapon for latent fingerprints, trace evidence, or blood. Most have to do with the operability of the weapon, its components, or its ammunition.

Operability

As mentioned at the beginning of this chapter, one of the important things related to firearms as evidence is whether a firearm works and is capable of operating as a firearm. Testing operability of a firearm is as simple as shooting it—after, of course, the weapon has been properly examined. You don't want it exploding in your face. Operability is determined by what is known as a test fire. And each time the weapon is test-fired, the bullet is recovered for possible additional testing or examination.

From the 1970s through 1992, when the police department moved to its new headquarters, the test fire of a firearm took place in a slender rectangular box about eight feet long. The box had a lid to allow for bullet retrieval, and the inside of the box was filled with old mattress innards. Every foot, a piece of paper was inserted to help make bullet recovery easier. We would find the last paper pierced by the bullet and the next one that was not pierced, then search the mattress fiber in that cubic foot until we found the bullet. In the last two feet at the end of the box, old telephone books were placed to help stop any bullet that passed through all of the mattress stuff. Interestingly, every few inches, the wooden planks of the box displayed little holes that resembled a popcorn explosion, giving testimony to the fact that the technician didn't hold the gun quite straight.

When the department moved to its new Beretania Street headquarters, the Scientific Investigation Section's firearm unit got its own lab and test-fire room. In addition, it got a brand new retrieval tank to test-fire firearms. This was a large tank filled with water. The weapon was fired into the water, and the theory was that the water would slow the bullet until it fell to the bottom of the tank. Several times, however, the bullet left an indentation in the back wall of the tank. The very first problem the technicians discovered was that the tank leaked. That old rectangular wooden box never did leak mattress fluff. It was low tech, but it worked.

Distance Determination

I asked for a short answer to the following question in one of my forensic/CSI classes: "Describe the procedure in conducting firearm distance determination." One student, who apparently missed the day it was discussed, wrote, "You shoot the gun parallel to the ground in a big field. Then you go find the bullet and measure the distance it traveled." This is *not* the correct answer!

When a person is shot at close range, smoke, soot, and unburned powder particles from the cartridge come flying out of the barrel. These fly forward and penetrate the victim's clothes and body. People sometimes call this action "powder burns." This is not correct. The unburned particles actually embed themselves in the cloth and create tiny lacerations on the victim's skin. The proper term is "stippling."

If we recover the weapon and can take a 1:1 photo of the stippling on the victim's skin and again of the soot pattern on the victim's clothing, we can try to reproduce that in the lab and thus estimate the approximate distance the weapon was held from the victim when it was fired.

The procedure is simple. The weapon is fixed to a stand and aimed level in the firearm lab. Clean white paper is hung on a pulley running horizontally above the gun at a distance of six inches. The gun is fired and the stippling and soot pattern is made on the white paper. This is repeated every six inches until a pattern emerges that is approximately the same size as the pattern on the victim and his clothing. We then simply measure the distance from gun to paper and we have the approximate distance of the gun from victim in the shooting.

I didn't have the heart to mark that student's answer wrong. His response was so sincere and childlike that I appreciated his fresh look at the problem.

Bullet Striation Comparison

The bores of firearms that are rifled have tiny imperfections on the surface of the metal. These imperfections, as small as they can be, are nevertheless made of much harder metal than the bullet of a cartridge, which is usually a lead alloy, sometimes with brass or copper jackets. As the bullet is pushed through the bore by the expanding gas of the burning gunpowder, it rubs over those tiny imperfections, which leave striation marks on the bullet. These striation marks will be the same for all bullets fired by the same firearm.

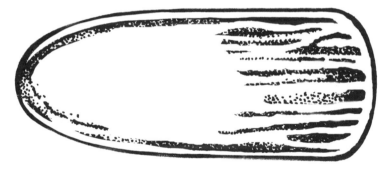

A striated bullet

If a bullet can be recovered from the body of a victim, for example, and a firearm is recovered when a suspect is arrested, the firearm can then be compared with a bullet recovered in a test fire of the same firearm. The evidence and the test-fired sample are then compared under a comparison microscope. A comparison microscope is actually two identical microscopes connected by an optical bridge. This enables the technician to view two objects side by side, with the capability to rotate both objects to see if they match. In this case, the technician rotates the two bullets to see if the striations on each bullet match. If they do, the evidence will be conclusive (direct evidence) that the bullet taken from the victim's body was fired from the gun that was in possession of the suspect at the time he was arrested. It does not prove, however, who fired the weapon.

Firing Pin Indentation/Ejector Mark Comparison

The comparison microscope is used again in comparing firing pin indentations and ejector marks on cartridges. The metal of each firing pin, like the metal of the bore, is harder material than that of the primer. When the firing pin strikes the primer, it leaves an indentation. This indentation on cartridges in evidence can be compared against test-fired samples.

The same testing can be done on cartridge ejection marks. In semiautomatic weapons, a metal ejector helps push the spent cartridge from the gun's chamber. This action leaves a mark on the cartridge, which can be compared with the firearm as were the bullet and firing pin described above. Again, a positive comparison is direct evidence and proves the evidence cartridge came from that semiautomatic firearm.

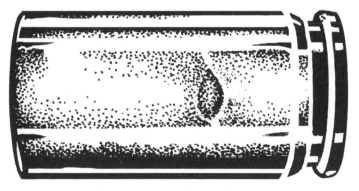

Cartridge striation marks

Velocity

Remember the war I declared on math? Your homework is to figure out how to calculate velocity. In the firearms lab, however, we have equipment to figure that out for math-challenged people like me. And it's easy, too. Two plastic triangles that emit magnetic fields, or space rays, or probably some force field or something having to do with math are set up opposite each other at a measured distance. A high-speed stopwatch/timer is part of the equipment. The firearm is fired from outside one triangle. When the bullet passes the first triangle, it breaks the force field and the stopwatch/timer starts. When it passes the second triangle, breaking the second magic field, the stopwatch/timer stops. The equipment then "tells" us the velocity of the bullet. It has something to do with distance and time, I'm told: multiplied, divided, added, subtracted—I dunno. That's your homework. Beam me up, Scotty!

Gunshot Residue Analysis

Remember that when a handgun is fired, the primer explodes and the particles from the primer come back toward the shooter through the openings in the frame at the cylinder and the hammer. These particles can collect on the back of the shooter's gun hand—particularly in the area between the thumb and index finger.

If the shooter is caught not long after the shooting, the technician uses a cylindrical disk with tacky glue on one end to daub the back side of the shooter's hand, collecting gunshot residue, as well as dust, sweat, and grime. This disk can later be analyzed using a scanning electron microscope, or SEM (which is not a true microscope at all). The SEM will present the technician with a readout identifying particles and their chemical makeup. If the particles prove to be chemicals associated with primer, it's good circumstantial evidence that the suspect fired a handgun.

Handling Firearms during Investigations

Before the public began its fascination with CSIs and forensic science, TV shows and movies often pictured the detective or crime scene investigator picking up a firearm by sticking a slender rod, like a pen, into the barrel. Never *ever* do that! It's a dumb cop who inserts anything into the barrel of a firearm that has been used in a shooting. Inserting something into the barrel can alter the imperfections

Pick up the firearm by its grip.

in the barrel and inadvertently cause striation comparison to be questioned. And since many of us use expensive Mont Blanc or Namiki pens, what a foolish thing to do—put a Namiki into the barrel of a gun!

Neither do you want to grab the firearm anywhere on its metal frame; even though some of the exposed metal surfaces are very small, it's still possible to lift fingerprints from them. In many instances, firearms will be searched for fingerprints by using the superglue method. This method is used on the gun's ammunition as well.

Nearly all firearms have a grip of sorts. And nearly all grips have crisscross or checkerboard patterns cut or imprinted in them. Prints cannot be obtained from a grip, so that's where investigators carefully grab and handle the weapon. They should always pick up the firearm by its grip at crime scenes.

Unloading the weapon can be an issue as well. Too many times we have seen inexperienced officers unloading firearms. When we ask them why, they respond, "It's loaded and dangerous." Yes, it's loaded, but who makes it dangerous? People forget that the firearm is not going to fire itself. And most gun manufacturers take great care to ensure that the weapon doesn't go off accidentally.

The unloading of a weapon at a crime scene should be left for the crime scene technician. The technician will ensure it is done safely and that all the information about the ammunition and chamber and/or cylinder positions is recorded. For example, it is important to learn the number of cartridges in a revolver recovered in a shooting, their position in the cylinder, and in which position any spent shells are located. There are many reasons for this, but primarily we want to see if the weapon was tampered with after the shooting. Different manufacturers make the cylinder in revolvers to rotate either clockwise or counterclockwise. A spent shell in the wrong side of the frame means someone tampered with the gun. Likewise, in a revolver, a single spent shell out of firing order in an alleged suicide will indicate tampering or an attempt to make a murder appear to be a suicide.

We had a case in which a crook was lying dead in his living room with a single gunshot to his head. In his hand was a revolver. His crook friends said that he was playing Russian roulette. Examination of the weapon's cylinder, however, showed that the spent shell was on the wrong side of the frame in relation to the cylinder's rotation. In addition, the dead guy had no gunshot residue on his hands. Also, the dead guy was right-handed, but the entry hole was in his left temple. We suspected fairly quickly that someone shot him, examined the weapon and in doing so turned the cylinder, and put it in his hand.

By the way, be really suspicious if you're told that the victim accidentally killed himself by playing Russian roulette with a semiautomatic pistol, since the automatic feature would remove any element of survival (unless, of course, the losing player in Russian roulette was a guy named Buster Babooze).

What if suspects are still around and the loaded gun is on the floor? Pick it up properly, if you have to keep it out of the hands of people who may use it to shoot you, and put it in the locked trunk of your car, after marking its location on the floor.

Spent shell casings need careful handling, too. Remember,

someone has to hold and handle those casings when they are inserted into the ammunition clip that goes into the semiautomatic handgun. Latent prints just might be waiting to be recovered. If you find spent shell casings on the floor, mark their locations with highly visible markers. Otherwise, people at the crime scene may accidentally step on one and crush it, destroying the chance for good latent recovery.

A Final Word

Members of the National Rifle Association (NRA) say, "Guns don't kill. People do." Remember old Ben Hur—Charlton Heston, aka Moses himself? (He won an Academy Award for at least one of those movies, I think.) He agrees. Guns are *lifeless* hunks of metal that just so happen to be the weapon most often used to take the *life* of an innocent person.

Well, I can tell you here, based on my twenty-seven years of experience with the Honolulu Police Department, six of which were as the lieutenant in charge of the Homicide Detail, that yes, people do kill, and yes, they use guns to kill most of the time. In fact, the Federal Bureau of Investigation (FBI) reports, based on the information they receive from police departments across the nation, that guns *are* the number one weapon used to kill people. So Charlton Heston is right, too—as long as people are the ones doing the killing. Any other animal group using guns to kill people doesn't count.

I can tell you also of the tragedy that occurs, also across the nation, when a child picks up a gun at home and accidentally kills another child—or himself or herself.

You can come to your own conclusion on whether guns or people kill. But I pray that if you have a gun in your home it's unloaded, its ammunition is separate from the weapon, it has a trigger lock, and it's secured in a case that is locked and impossible for a child to get into.

Don't let a child—perhaps your child—become a statistic for the FBI.

Firearms Experiment #1

Oops—hold on a minute! There aren't any experiments you can conduct in your home involving the shooting of a firearm. I don't want anyone to accidentally hurt himself or someone else by playing with a firearm.

I'll say again that all firearms in the home should have a cylinder lock or a trigger guard lock, and the weapon should be secured out of the reach of children or persons not authorized to touch it. Safety must rule.

So, instead of an experiment here, I'll give you a little quiz.

Print your name: _____

Spelling counts.

Answer all questions:

1. Caliber is measured in feet.

a. True   b. False

2. The bullet is

a. The cartridge that goes into the revolver.

b. the lead projectile that is the tip of the cartridge.

c. a can of beer.

3. Reading *Honolulu Cop* and *Honolulu Homicide* is a good primer for this book.

a. True   b. True

Send this back to me for grading. You get extra credit if you include a photocopy of your receipt for *Honolulu Cop* and *Honolulu Homicide*.

6
Arson and Explosives

Take a newspaper, crumple the pages, and place them in the corner of a room. Get a paper cup of gasoline and pour it over the newspapers. Open a book of cardboard matches. Light the book and throw it on the pile of crumpled newspapers. Soon the fire will be crawling up the wall, spreading a thick black smoke along the ceiling. In a few minutes the fire will be large enough to engulf the room. A few minutes more and the temperature will reach 1,000 to 1,500 degrees Fahrenheit. At the same time as the oxygen in the room is used up, a pulsating backdraft breathes flames out of doors, and windows are blown outward. No one can survive at this point in the fire. All this is the result of a newspaper, a cup of gasoline, and a book of matches.

"And no one gets caught," you say. "It's the perfect crime—all the evidence is burned to ashes and dust."

OXYGEN

FUEL　　　　　**HEAT**

Wrong, Sherlock. A good arson investigator—and the police and fire departments have excellent ones—will be able to find exactly where you set the fire, how you set it, and whether you used flammable material to accelerate the fire during ignition.

Remember your third-grade teacher telling you that you needed three things in order for a fire to exist? It was called the "Fire Triangle." In order for combustion—aka a fire—to exist, it needs oxygen. Pretty much, that's all around us. Then it needs fuel. That can be anything from crumpled newspapers to gasoline-soaked wood. Last, it needs heat. This can be a lit match or simply the heat of the sun.

Phases of a Fire

If a fire were to start in your kitchen while you were cooking, it is likely that you would put it out very quickly. But if a fire were to start in your home while you were out, it would probably go through different phases before the firefighters were able to extinguish it.

Phase 1: The Incipient Phase

In this phase, the fire is young and there is still a lot of oxygen in the air. Here the fire is producing water vapor, carbon dioxide, and a small quantity of carbon monoxide. Heat is being generated and will increase as the fire continues. The temperature of the flames may rise to well above 1,000 degrees, while the temperature of the surrounding room may rise only slightly.

Phase 2: The Free-Burning Phase

This phase incorporates all of the free-burning action of the fire. Oxygen-rich air is drawn into the flames and carries heat into the ceiling area of the room. This occurs through the convection process, in just the same manner as it does in your oven. The heated gases spread outward and down, forcing the cooler air to the ground. This explains why the advice given to escape a fire is to drop down and crawl to safety. The air has now heated to between 1,300 and

1,500 degrees. One breath of this superheated air can sear and burn your lungs to an irreparable condition. Very soon, all of the materials that can burn will catch on fire. The flames continue to consume oxygen until they reach the point where there is not enough oxygen to continue the burning. The fire goes into a smoldering phase. All that's needed now is an addition of oxygen and the fire will explode into a pulsating back draft.

Phase 3: The Smoldering Phase

Here, if the room is airtight, the flame will cease to exist and the fire will go into the smoldering phase. The flames are reduced to glowing embers. The room is filled with superheated smoke and gases, which causes the pressure to become greater and greater. The intense heat will have vaporized some gases that were produced from burning material, and the possibility of a back draft becomes dangerously high.

Phase 4: Backdraft

Firefighters responding to a fire that is in the smoldering phase risk a backdraft when they open an access to the room. When oxygen is supplied, by simply opening a door or window, the unburned carbon particles can combust instantaneously, creating tremendously devastating pulsating explosions. Anything still alive in that room dies long before that moment.

Arson Investigation

Perhaps the biggest problem associated with arson investigation is that much of the evidence has been burned. Then firefighters have doused it with untold gallons of water and perhaps trampled the scene in their efforts to extinguish the flames. Nevertheless, it is certainly quite possible to successfully investigate arson and to apprehend and convict those people responsible.

Often a fire is set to hide other crimes, which frequently is the case with murder. Other fires are started for insurance claims by those who want to collect money. The fire investigator needs to focus on several things to be successful.

- *Where?* Where did the fire start? A number of signs among the debris will help the fire investigator determine where in the burned-out building the fire was started.
- *What?* What, if anything, was used to start the fire?
- *Why?* Why was the fire started? In other words, what was the motive of the offense?
- *Who?* Who started it, if it was not accidental?
- *How?* How was the fire started?

As with any offense, these key questions can be answered mostly through the physical evidence gathered in the CSI. And one of the first steps is to determine where the fire started. This is done by finding the location that exhibits the most deeply burned area, which in turn can be found through several indicators.

The Inverted Cone

The origin of the fire, if started against a wall, will show a burn pattern resembling an inverted cone, like an ice cream cone with the point on the bottom. (Finish your ice cream before turning your cone over to check this statement.) This indicator can frequently be found with other evidence of arson, such as charred rags piled in one corner.

Spalling

Spalling is the chipping or splintering of tile, concrete, or cinder blocks as a result of an intense hot spot, often found at the fire's origin.

Depth of Char

At the point of origin of a fire, the fire will have been burning for a greater time than other locations. The depth of char, or how deep into wood the char has occurred, can assist in pinpointing the location where the fire started.

Alligatoring

"Alligatoring" is the term used to describe the surface texture of burned wood, because it looks like the skin of an alligator. The location where alligatoring is most intense can be an indicator of the origin of the fire.

Igniters

Investigators need to search debris for devices that can be used to ignite a fire. The wide variety of igniters includes gunpowder, matches, and electronic gadgets, to name a few. Also, at places of origin the investigators need to look for delay devices. A very simple delay device can be created with a matchbook, a cigarette, and a clothespin. Attach an exposed matchbook an inch from the end of the cigarette with the clothespin, ensuring that the match heads are touching the cigarette. Light the cigarette and it will burn down slowly. When it reaches the matchbook, it will ignite the matches and create a flame for a minute or so. Place this device adjacent to paper soaked in a flammable liquid and when it flames, you have the ignition for your arson fire. The problem for the arsonist is that the device, as with other ignition devices, rarely burns completely away, which leaves evidence for the investigator to recover.

Fire Deaths

Unfortunately, in some cases people die in fires. Most of these deaths occur as a result of smoke inhalation, not by burning in the fire. When people—children especially—become trapped in a fire, they try to hide away from the flames if they cannot reach doors or windows and when the smoke envelops the room, they suffocate because of the lack of air. If you have young children and you are ever involved in a fire—and we pray you never are—look for them under beds and in closets. They will hide from the fire. And sadly, many children who die in fires are found under beds and in closets.

It's important to know whether the person whose body was found at the scene of a fire died during the fire or before the fire. When a person dies during the fire, the ME will find soot and ash in the deceased's mouth, esophagus, and lungs. This tells us that the dead person was breathing during the fire and inhaling soot and ash. If the soot and ash are missing, that indicates that the person was dead before the fire.

We had a case in which the body of a woman was found in a closet after firefighters extinguished a roaring fire that burned down her home. Her body was completely charred. During autopsy, the ME told us that the woman died before the fire. There was no soot in her mouth, esophagus, or lungs. This caused the ME to search for another cause of death, and he found it. She had been stabbed in the heart. The arson investigator also helped by determining that the fire had been deliberately set. What we did not expect was that when we attempted to speak to members of her family, they refused to speak to us and wanted to see an attorney. Well, now—these are things that make you more than a little suspicious.

Explosives

Most people don't know that there is a difference between explosives. That most explosives go *bang* when they go off and that you can get hurt is about all they need to know. And for most people, that's good enough. But CSI junkies have to know that explosives are grouped into two classifications: low explosives and high explosives. Low explosives burn rapidly. High explosives explode. The damage caused by low explosives is a result of the force of the expanding gas caused by burning. Because of this, low explosives need to be confined to "explode"—the expanding gas exerts great pressure on its container until the container bursts apart. High explosives, on the other hand, are normally detonated by shock and have much greater velocities when exploded. This means you get a bigger bang for your bomb.

Low Explosives

Perhaps the best example of a low explosive is a bullet cartridge with black powder. When ignited by the primer, the black powder burns rather than explodes, and the rapidly expanding gas causes the bullet to "explode" free from the shell casing. Pipe bombs are also constructed with low explosives. The powder is compacted into the pipe, then the cover is screwed on. This is the reason that people lose hands and fingers during construction of a pipe bomb. Any friction may create a spark and *bang!* Say hello to Eight-Fingered Bobby. Low explosives such as black powder are sensitive to heat, impact, and friction, in addition to sparks.

Commercially manufactured safety fuses are usually what an experienced pipe bomber uses to detonate his device. These fuses normally burn at a rate of one foot every thirty seconds or so. The safety fuse is made up of black powder wrapped by cotton yarn, a waterproofing material, and an outer covering, sometimes of a wax-coated yarn.

COMMERCIAL SAFETY FUSE

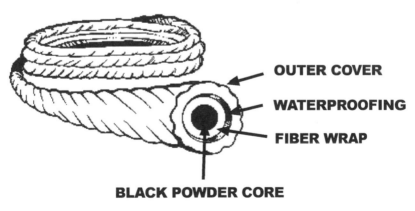

OUTER COVER

WATERPROOFING

FIBER WRAP

BLACK POWDER CORE

A typical safety fuse

High Explosives

High explosives are also called "primary" explosives. These explode with heat or shock, and the best example is the primer used to detonate bullet cartridges. Examples of such explosives are nitro-glycerine, dynamite, and ammonium nitrate. Ammonium nitrate is also used as a fertilizer, but it is a less pure form than the explosive. Fertilizer, you may recall, was used as part of the car bomb in the Oklahoma City federal building bombing.

In 1992, when the Honolulu Police Department was moving from the Pāwaʻa Annex building (an old Sears store) to its new site at 801 S. Beretania Street, I had been recently promoted to the captain-in-charge of the Scientific Investigation Section. On one of the moving days, one of our evidence technicians called out to me after he opened a drawer in one of our labs.

"Captain, try come."

"What?"

"Look at this."

"Is that what I think it is?"

"Yup."

I was looking at a stick of dynamite and it was "sweating"—in other words, it was unstable. I had visions of my brand-new badge being blown to tiny little globs of molten metal. Our SWAT team came, agreed that the dynamite was unstable, and called the army's Explosive Ordnance Detail, which came and removed it. In *Honolulu Cop,* I described how, many years before, I almost burned down the Kāneʻohe police station. If that dynamite had gone off, can you imagine the chapter that would have made? As it was, the conversation with my boss went something like this:

"You found what?"

"A stick of dynamite."

"You found *what?*"

"Dynamite. It was at the back of a drawer that no one used."

"You found WHAT?"

Shock is the best way I can describe his demeanor. And nothing I could say alleviated his surprise and apparent apprehension in having to tell *his* boss about that extraordinarily dangerous situation—in a desk, in the police station.

Bomb Investigation

The requirements for the crime scene of a bomb explosion are much like those of any other crime scene, with one exception: the search. A spiral search is used, starting at the seat of the explosion—the precise location where the bomb was detonated. This search pattern should continue outward until the last fragment is found, and then it should be extended at least a distance halfway more than from the seat of the explosion to the farthest fragment. This is to ensure that nothing is left behind.

Spiral search at a bomb scene

These investigations focus on finding fragments of the material used to construct the bomb. These fragments can serve as evidence of MO, in the event of a series of explosions occurring, and to possibly learn where these parts were obtained. At times, the nature of the parts of the bomb, even if they're broken and torn to bits, can lead investigators to specific manufacturers of such parts. And when combined with the identity of a possible suspect, this information can help provide identification of the person responsible for the bombing.

A key element in the investigation is the witness. Witnesses can perhaps describe the person who placed the device. Finding that person, however, can be just as difficult as finding tiny bits of debris spread out across the scene of a bombing.

Expect confusion at a bomb scene, especially if people are hurt. But once the scene is contained and secured, the processing should be deliberate and painstaking. The exploded device may leave tiny fragments that could easily be overlooked.

Television and movie bomb scenes do not represent reality. But it's okay to practice the line "Nothing to see here—move along, move along!"

A Final Word

There is not enough praise or thanks we can give to those men and women who risk their lives every day by fighting fires, responding to disasters or dangerous conditions to rescue people, or simply responding to calls for help. Whether you are firefighters, police officers, or an everyday Joe or Jane who goes into a burning building to save someone else—thank you!

Arson Experiment #1: Does the Flame Really Go Out?

Equipment:

1. Tapered candle secured in a safe base

2. Wooden kitchen matches

Secure the candle in a holder with a wide base and ensure that it does not tip over. With a kitchen match, light the candle.

Extinguish the match—not with your fingers, babooze.

Allow the candle to burn for a few seconds to establish a fully developed flame. Light a second match. Blow out the candle. No, not the match—the candle.

Bring the second lit match to about one-quarter inch over the top of the extinguished candle's wick.

The flame should rekindle itself on the wick, without ever touching the lit match to the extinguished wick. Neat, huh?

What occurs is that the fuel, which was in the form of a solid wax-coated wick, has been turned into gaseous form. That gas fuel, combined with the surrounding air and the heat supplied by the flame of the second match, reignited the wick without ever touching it.

If this didn't work, you must have bad air. Or maybe you didn't light the second match. Either way, try not to get burned—and no burn your house!

Explosives Experiment #1

None, absolutely nothing—nope, no experiment—nada. Don't do anything in conjunction with explosives in this chapter that will cause you to burn yourself or your loved ones, explode your house or your dog, lose fingers and hands, or kill yourself or someone else. You hear?

Therefore, you'll get test #2.

Name:

_____

Print your legal name, not the one you give to process servers.
Answer all questions:

1. Fire gets hot after a second or so.
a. True   b. False
2. Homemade explosives tend to blow off fingers and hands.
a. Damn true   b. False
3. Reading *Honolulu Cop* and *Honolulu Homicide* is a good primer for this book.
a. True   b. True

Send this back to me for grading. You get extra credit if you include a picture of you holding your copies of *Honolulu Cop* and *Honolulu Homicide*. And if you blew off your fingers playing with explosives, make sure we can see that in the photo and we'll use you in our next book: *Honolulu Babooze*.

7
Impression Evidence

"Impression evidence" is a general term for any type of evidence that was created by contact with another object or substance. (It's not like the kind of "good impression" you get when you meet someone for the first time.) Primarily, there are two broad categories of impression evidence: evidence created via *compression* and evidence created by *compression and scraping* known as *striation marks*.

Compression evidence requires some degree of force in a perpendicular motion to the object receiving the compression. The object receiving the force must be soft enough or malleable enough to receive the impression of the firmer object pushing onto it. That's a rather fancy definition of a shoeprint, for example.

Another common type of compression evidence is the tire track. One important aspect to remember is that when you look at compression evidence, you're looking at the reverse of the object—that is, the higher levels or ridges of the object are the lower levels or grooves in the surface or substance receiving the compression.

Striation evidence requires not only a perpendicular force but a parallel sliding as well. This is best seen in the striation marks left on bullets that have passed through the rifled bore of a firearm.

Examples of Impression Evidence

Foot Impression

A footprint can be used to show identity in the same way as a fingerprint, with ridges that can be compared to those of a suspect. Therefore the proper term for that *impression* by a *foot* is—you guessed it—a "foot impression," to avoid confusing it with a footprint.

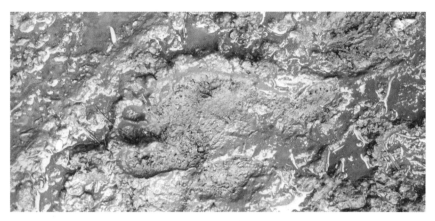

Example of a foot impression

Foot impressions can be found at many crime scenes in Hawai'i. The value of foot impressions left in dirt or mud is that they give an indication of the size of the foot that left them. Inference can then be made as to the height of the person leaving the impression, remembering that it is inference only. In addition, the foot impression in soft material can also show evidence of injuries or scars or irregularities of the foot and toes. When left on a smooth, hard surface, it has the same value as fingerprints, and positive identification is possible when compared with the culprit.

Shoeprints

A shoeprint in soft material can provide a great deal of information. Like a footprint, shoeprints can identify size of the shoe, a heel or sole pattern, which may also show wear and erosion, and perhaps even the manufacturer's brand name. There was a murder in downtown Honolulu in which the body of a partially dressed transvestite was found in an alleyway near a bar. The victim appeared to have been beaten to death. Across the victim's chest was what looked like the impression of the sole of a shoe with a tread pattern and the letters of the company's name. Our evidence specialists took 1:1 photos of that impression and we sent a copy of the photo to the manufacturer. The company wrote back to us saying that the particular tread

Example of a shoeprint

pattern of the evidence belonged to a specific shoe manufactured at a specific plant in San Diego and was sold to stores in the Southern California area. That information added to our suspicion that the killer was a sailor. The fleet was in, so to speak, at Pearl Harbor on the night of the murder, and several thousand sailors were on shore leave. Witnesses told us that the victim, dressed as a woman, was in the company of several young men who resembled the "military type." They also told us that he left the bar with the men but did not return. We suspected that the victim and the men went to the alley for prostitution activities, and when the men learned that their companion was not female, they beat him to death—one of them stomping on the victim's chest.

Tire Tracks

Like shoes, tires leave tread impressions in the soft material over which they roll. These impressions will show wear and tear of the tread along with tiny imperfections in the tire rubber. Photos on a 1:1 basis are taken of tire tracks, as with shoeprints. The impression (shoeprints and tire tracks alike) should also be cast with dental stone, a fine material similar to plaster of paris.

The body of a man was found in tall brush alongside a dirt roadway in 'Ewa. He had been shot in the head. Across one leg and in the

Example of tire tracks

muddy roadway were tire tracks. Photos were taken and a casting was made of the tread track in the mud. These prints showed us that the tire that ran over the victim's leg and the one in the mud were from different tires. A few days later, a suspect was identified and arrested and his vehicle was seized and processed. We took inked prints of the vehicle's tires and made positive comparisons of two of the vehicle's tires with the impressions left on the dead man's leg and in the mud, proving that the suspect's vehicle was associated with the killing.

Tire tracks in dirt have proved time and again to be extremely useful in criminal investigations. When a vehicle drives forward in a straight line in soft dirt, the tracks it leaves are those of its two rear tires, since the last impression is the rear tires, and usually that last impression covers over the tracks left by the front tires. It's the opposite when the vehicle is driving in reverse—the tracks left belong to the front tires. It's when the vehicle makes a turn that you can usually see all four tire tracks.

It must be noted that when the police recover tire track impression evidence and they locate a suspect vehicle, the sample they take

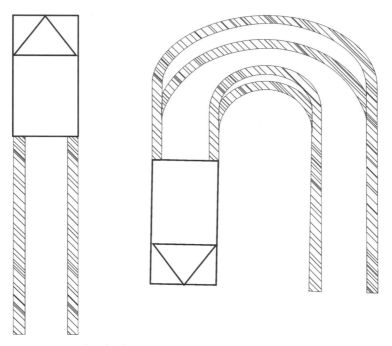

Tracks of vehicle moving in a straight line and in a turn

from that suspect vehicle must be taken while the tire is inflated and on the car. The tread of a tire removed from the vehicle will be rounded because there is no weight pushing it to the ground. The sample must be taken as it existed at the scene.

A young man who was suspected of dealing in drugs was abducted from his residence. A week later his body was found down a ravine off a harvested pineapple field. At the time, it was presumed he was murdered because of his suspected illegal drug activities. During the examination of the crime scene where the body was found, many tire tracks were found. The beautiful thing was that the tire tracks helped to reconstruct the following scenario: The suspect vehicle drove into the field, made a U-turn, and backed up to the ravine; then someone dumped his body down the slope of the ravine. The dirt was only semi-soft over most of the area, with few sites where some of the tire tread could be seen—except for a six-foot area where all four tire tracks of the suspect vehicle converged after it completed its turn. This was an exceptional piece of luck, because all four tires had different treads. The implication was that if we found the vehicle, we would have very strong evidence that it was the vehicle used to dump the body.

What followed was an incident of outrageous proportions. After the detective instructed the technician to photograph and cast all four tracks, the technician, who apparently was upset at being ordered to do duplicate work, photographed and cast only one of the tracks and destroyed the others by smearing them with his feet. What he didn't realize was that another officer witnessed him destroying the tracks. We couldn't prove whether his intent was malicious, as he claimed that he believed he was doing duplicate work. But he was fired from his job for a multitude of reasons, primarily for failing to follow orders, failing to follow evidentiary procedures, and deliberately destroying evidence, even though his intent was not malicious.

Bite Marks

Whether animal or human, bite marks—the impression of teeth left in skin or any other material capable of holding that impression—are excellent items of evidence. These marks can often be found in Styrofoam cups, cheese, and certain fruit. In the case of a human biting another human, that bite mark can sometimes be compared so precisely that positive identification can be made between the bite marks and the teeth that made them.

We find bite marks in many violent criminal offenses. Unarmed people fighting for their lives will often bite their attackers. In fact, when I lecture about the prevention of violence and protecting yourself, I tell people that when their life is threatened, they should do anything to stop the attack and escape—kick, punch, scream, and bite their attacker. Bite as hard as you possibly can.

Bite marks are also found on victims. In both physical and sexual assault cases, suspects have been known to bite their victims. These bite marks need to be processed properly to obtain the most accurate representation of the injury possible.

The first effort in documenting bite marks is to photograph them. The photography must be done on a 1:1 basis to obtain the accurate size of the mark. Additional 35 mm photos should be taken for documentation. The photos should be taken in both color and black and white from a perpendicular position to the wound.

One photo session isn't enough. Bite marks continue to develop over a few days, both on living and dead victims. The photo series should be taken daily. Bruises will develop and it may just be that the bite mark photos taken on day three will be the best for comparison purposes.

Bite marks may consist of bruises only or both bruises and lacerations. In many cases, a bite mark that appears very faint or an old bite mark whose bruises have faded may be seen more clearly with the use of ultraviolet light. This helps to highlight the bruising that remains under the outer layer of skin. Photography can then be used to "capture" the bite mark on film.

In some cases where indentations to the skin occur, the bite mark can also be cast with dental stone casting material. The forensic odontologist will perform this casting using his or her expertise to obtain a hard-cast replica of the bite in the victim's skin. The odontologist will also take a cast of a suspect's teeth in the same manner as one would do in the preparation of dental bridges or braces. Once the cast of the suspect's teeth is made and has hardened, it is placed against the photo of the bite mark. Teeth are so unique in size, spacing, and shape that when the cast is placed over the photo of the bite mark, it sometimes fits exactly, providing positive identification of the suspect as the person who bit the victim.

Tool Marks

Perhaps the most commonly known tool marks are the impressions left in doorknobs after a burglar tries to break the locking mechanism by forcing the knob with a pair of pliers. These and other marks (made by knives, axes, screwdrivers, and crowbars) are identifiable particularly when the tools have imperfections that can be traced back to an individual tool.

A Final Word

Finally, impression evidence will leave you with the impression that impressions into material that can accept impressions are merely circumstantial evidence used to impress the jury. Huh?

Don't get the wrong impression.

Impression Evidence Experiment #1: Tire Tread Examination

Equipment:
1. Black ink or paint
2. A vehicle with tires
3. White 8 1/2" x 11" paper
4. A partner

Ask your partner to get into the vehicle and wait for instructions. Please make sure that your partner has a valid driver's license and knows how to drive. Make sure also that there is more than six feet of clear driveway, garage, and so on, so the vehicle won't collide with anything.

Set a clean sheet of paper on the ground in front of a front tire, making sure the edge of the paper is touching the tire where the tire contacts the driveway. Use the black ink or paint and paint the tire tread about one inch off the ground and upward for about six inches.

Move away from the vehicle. Tell your partner to start the car, put it into drive, and move very slowly forward until the tire has completely rolled over the paper.

Yell, "Stop! Turn off the car!"

If the car runs over your hand, yell, "Stop! Put the car in reverse!"

Retrieve the paper and examine the inked tire track. Look for the tiny imperfections that are not noticeable during normal activity. These imperfections are what make the comparison good evidence.

If all you get is the impression of your very flat hand, switch places with your partner.

Impression Evidence Experiment #2: Casting a Shoeprint
Equipment:
1. Running shoes
2. Plaster of paris
3. Shoe box or four lengths of wood 1" x 1/2" x 1"
4. Can of hairspray (if you're a guy, borrow one from your honey)
5. Several strips or squares of gauze

Put on the shoes. Find a spot in your yard that is only dirt. Fine, dusty dirt is better than hard, claylike soil. Using your garden hose, wet the dirt until you have soft mud.

Carefully step onto the muddy area, applying a gentle straight-down pressure. (Yes, we know that's not how you would normally be walking, but this is an experiment. Give us a break, won't ya?) Allow the mud to dry a little—enough so there are no pockets of water and the mud has accepted and is holding the shoe-tread pattern.

Cut the bottom out of the shoebox or create a rectangle with the wood in a similar shape to the shoebox. Use this "frame" or "dam" and place it over the shoeprint, ensuring that the print is clearly visible inside this dam frame (hold on, did I just say that?). Spray the print with hairspray. Wait a minute and spray again. Do this six or so times, allowing the hairspray to dry thoroughly. The hairspray helps to hold up the fine ridges of the print.

Following the instructions on the box of plaster of paris, mix about a quart of mixture, but then add a little more water to make it just a little thin. Carefully pour the mixture into the shoeprint. Cover the entire print and stop when the mixture reaches the level of the ground. At this point, lay down a layer of gauze. The gauze acts like wire in concrete and helps to hold the plaster of paris together and keep it from cracking.

Continue to pour the remainder of the mixture into the dam frame, filling up as much as you can to the edges of the frame. Allow it to dry for several hours.

When you remove the cast, you should be able to clean the dirt away and clearly see the image of your shoeprint. If you can't—wow, brah, I don't know what to say.

Impression Evidence Experiment #3: Bite Marks
Equipment:
1. Your teeth
2. Slice of American cheese
3. Piece of clean paper
4. Pencil

Carefully bite on the slice to create an impression, making sure not to bite through it. This represents the bite mark on a victim— the evidence.

Push the clean paper with your fingers against your upper teeth. Take the pencil and darken the impressions made onto the paper. This represents the image or casting made of the suspect by an odontologist.

Lay the cheese down on a clean surface. Lay the paper down on the cheese and carefully manipulate it until you can see the darkened impressions "fit" over the impressions on the cheese.

You should be able to see the match between the evidence and the sample. If this doesn't work, give up and eat the cheese.

Impression Evidence Experiment #4: Tool Marks
Equipment:
1. Lead fishing weight, at least six ounces
2. Three to six pairs of pliers
3. Magnifying glass
4. Silly Putty
5. A partner

Give your partner the pairs of pliers and the fishing lead. Instruct him or her to go into the next room and, when alone, to select one pair of pliers, open the pliers to the wide position, and then, with as much pressure as he or she can muster, squeeze the pliers and imprint the lead piece with the ridges and grooves of the pliers' teeth.

Now have your partner bring back the lead fishing weight and the various pliers and give them all to you. The impression on the lead weight is in reverse to the pliers, so get the Silly Putty and push it onto the impression on the lead weight. The impression should now be in the same view and orientation as the ridges of the teeth on the pliers' head.

Using the magnifying glass, attempt to compare the impressions on the Silly Putty against the heads of the various pliers.

If you cannot, your partner cheated and used more than one pair of pliers.

8
Documents

Then there's the story about the world's dumbest bank robber. He enters the bank, pulls out his checkbook, tears off a deposit slip, and writes a demand note.

"I have a gun. Give me all your money."

The bank teller follows the procedures she's been taught and slides the note off the counter, allowing it to fall to the floor as she hands the robber some of the money in her tray—a bunch of ones and a few fives.

Later that afternoon, detectives arrest the robber at his house after getting his address off his deposit slip.

"Gee, brah, how you knew was me?" asks the bewildered crook.

"Cause we good, brah," comes the sarcastic reply.

Another bank robber hands the teller the demand note. It's written on a plain white piece of paper torn from a notebook. He takes the money and flees. But like his not-too-smart friend, he, too, is in custody within a few days. An indentation examination was conducted on the note and detectives found that the paper held impressions of the note written on the page just above it. The indentations read:

1979 Olds Cutlass
good condition
asking $1200
John, 333-1234

It was the information the robber wrote in the notebook just before he called it in to the newspaper to place an ad in the classifieds to sell his car.

If only they were all that easy; but they're not. And sometimes you need a little more examination of documents to get the information you need to solve the case.

There are several general categories of document investigation that help police investigators: document examination, ink examination, and handwriting analysis.

Document Examination

When you think of document examination, you may think of two common crimes: forgery and counterfeiting. Some people believe that forgery is as old as writing. In some forgery cases, we may see phony signatures used in an attempt to cash a stolen check. Forgery in the minds of many people means the altering of a signature or other writing. But another example is a thief who makes no effort to duplicate the signature of the original writer but writes the entire stolen check himself. It may also be the alteration of a document by typing over the original letters.

Counterfeiting is the attempt to produce a document that looks like the original document. This can be done as simply as using a photocopy machine or as professionally as using printing machines, exact quality of paper, and identical ink. This second type of counterfeiting can be seen in efforts to produce fake diplomas from a prestigious university, for example.

The counterfeiting we're most familiar with is good old U.S. currency. We see this a lot in old movies. But in real life, counterfeiters can make a phony twenty-dollar bill look just like the real thing. This is one of the reasons that the new twenty-dollar bill has multiple colors: to make it just a little more difficult to reproduce phony ones.

"Why the twenty?" you ask.

Well, one-dollar bills don't give the counterfeiter much return for his effort, and people just don't use hundreds as often as they use twenties. As a result, we see twenty-dollar bill counterfeits much more frequently than other bills. They are common enough not to stand out and provide enough return to make it worthwhile for the crook to counterfeit.

The U.S. Secret Service is the agency responsible for the investigation of counterfeiting of U.S. currency. It's not an easy task. If a cashier doing a count of money while closing a cash register notices that one twenty-dollar bill looks "funny," the local police will recover it and get the Secret Service involved. They'll recover the bill and ask their lab to examine it and see if there are any identical bills like it across the country. Remember, money that we get in Hawai'i may have also been used in any other U.S. state. For example, a businesswoman in Delaware uses a counterfeit twenty-dollar bill to purchase a notepad at a stationery store. An employee of the store buys a pen and uses a hundred dollar bill, telling his supervisor he needs the change for his upcoming trip to Disneyland. His supervisor says okay, and he gets four twenty-dollar bills as part of his change. He goes to Disneyland and has a great time, except for the headache he gets from his kids nagging him to ride Splash Mountain for a sixth time. On his last day, he leaves a twenty-dollar bill on the dresser of his hotel room. The maid, who gets the bill, is working her last day at the hotel as her husband is transferring to the Hawaiian Electric Company on O'ahu. The maid and her family arrive and she uses the twenty to pay for the cab ride from the airport. The cab driver uses the twenty to buy lunch at Zippy's. Later that night, the Zippy's clerk reconciles the day's receipts and the bill is taken to the bank the next day. The bank clerk, while counting the money, notices that the face on the twenty-dollar bill is Bill Clinton's and calls the Honolulu Police Department. The twenty went from Delaware to Hawai'i in less than a week.

There's actually a Web site where you can track U.S. paper money. Just log on to www.wheresgeorge.com. It's a site where people mark their bills by putting a red circle around George Washington's head. Then they register the denomination, series, and serial number on the site. The next step is to simply use the bills. Later they can check to see if their bills were ever found by anyone else who knew of and logged the bills into the Internet site. It's not illegal to mark the bills with the circle, but there have been instances in which the red circle has been inaccurately read by computer registers and identified as counterfeit, causing an investigation to begin.

Paper Examination

Investigators look at documents and examine paper quality, typing or handwriting, and ink. They look for similarities between the evidence and "known" samples. A known sample can be a document that investigators are certain was written or prepared by the suspect. Once the known sample and suspect are identified, investigators can then recover the machine or instrument used to make the known sample—a typewriter, for example. Using the known machine, investigators can then look for the imperfections of the machine, which should also be on the known sample. The examination might result in a positive comparison between the known sample and the known machine or instrument. Comparison can then be made between both the machine and sample against the evidence—direct proof that the instrument or machine was used to create the evidence document, perhaps tying the suspect to the instrument or machine.

Ink Examination

Ink can also be examined. Inks are made up of different pigments or chemicals, depending on who manufactures the ink. There are even different shades of the same color. A black ink, for example, is not simply black. Closer examination using ultraviolet light can show differences in the ink color.

A crook who forges an already made document will be using a different ink than was used by the original maker of the document. The crook may have stolen a check made out to cash for six dollars. The crook alters the check by changing the numerical amount to *60* and the written amount to *sixty* dollars. The investigator can then check on the different inks used to alter the check, proving the forgery.

Handwriting Examination

The crook in the example above endorses the check, signing a phony name to cash it. Investigators somehow identify a potential suspect. As part of their investigation, they then obtain a handwriting *exemplar*. Exemplars are handwriting samples provided by the suspect. In obtaining an exemplar, investigators will have the suspect write the phony name multiple times, perhaps twenty, thirty, or forty times. The reason for this is that it's expected the suspect will attempt to hide his true writing style by deliberately changing it— until his hand gets tired, that is. As we repeatedly write the same altered sentence or name, our hands will get tired and we will unconsciously revert to our natural writing style.

This exemplar is then examined by the investigator. He will look for similarities between the evidence and the suspect's writing samples. He will look for similarities such as letter formation, the slant of the letters and/or words, and the spacing between letters. There is also a technique known as "top of letter" and "bottom of letter" comparisons, which you can try in an experiment at the end of this chapter. Top of letter and bottom of letter comparisons look at similarities between the height of the letters of both samples, from bottom to top.

The handwriting exemplar

Whenever we write on paper in a notepad, the pressure on the paper causes the paper to be indented. This indentation extends below the top page. Depending on how hard the pressure is, this indentation can go as deep as six or seven pages. Whenever a note is recovered as evidence, that sheet of paper must be examined for indentation analysis. This process is not difficult but needs a special instrument. The note is placed on a flat surface of the machine and covered with a plastic-wrap material. An electronic charge is applied to the plastic-covered paper. This charge causes the plastic to be pulled tightly onto the paper and into the grooves of any indentation. The examiner then sprinkles a fine carbon powder onto the plastic. The instrument can then be set to vibrate at a very fast rate of speed. The powder then settles—or should—into the grooves of the inden- tation. The flat surface that the paper is resting on is then tilted so that the excess powder slides off, leaving only the powder in the grooves. A sticky paper, specifically manufactured for this purpose, is then placed on top of the plastic. This causes the plastic to adhere to the sticky paper, and the original note can be preserved without any damage to it during the process. What remains, in the form of the powder, is the writing that was on the notepad above the suspect paper.

A husband reported his wife missing. The police made a report, but she was not found. A week went by and the chief of police received a letter that described how the woman had a boyfriend. She and the boyfriend got into an argument. The letter said that the argu- ment became very heated and the boyfriend strangled the woman; he then took her body to a ditch in the country and left her there. The letter was allegedly written by the boyfriend, who expressed his remorse for the killing and wanted her body to be found. The letter was written on yellow legal-pad paper. Detectives recovered a notepad that was in the dead woman's home. An indentation analy- sis was done, and the detectives discovered that the letter sent to the chief of police was written on that very notepad. When confronted with this evidence, the suspect confessed to murdering his wife.

This case is an example of the fact that sometimes, no matter how much you plan or how confident you are that you can hide your crime, forensic science will find you out.

Paper Analysis

The paper we write on has varied differences depending on the manufacturer. These differences can be in fibers, tint, and ink, if the paper is ruled. Another really obvious difference occurs when paper is homemade. The fiber content can be very obvious in such papers.

But writing paper is not the only object made of paper. Matchbooks, also made of paper, can be analyzed. When a match is torn from the book and used in a crime, that match can be analyzed to see if it "matches" the book from which it came. Of course, this is useful only when the suspect apprehended has a book of matches in his possession. Investigators can examine the fibers in the recovered match against the recovered matchbook. They can also examine the tint and chemical content of the head of the match.

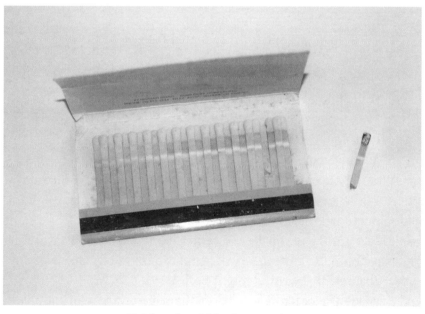

Match and matchbook comparison

A Final Word

One day when I was the captain-in-charge of the Scientific Investigation Section, I got a call from a woman who was a teacher at a Honolulu middle school. She was concerned that someone altered her grade report book. She told me that she was almost certain that little Billy was receiving a D in her math class. When she was preparing her grade sheet, there was a "B" in the line for his name. I told her to bring the grade sheet and come see us. She did. I looked at the grade sheet with a bright light and told her she didn't need to have the document examined any further, and I showed her the document again. You could clearly see that the ink color was different on the line that made the "D" a "B." She asked if I would see the student together with her and his parents. We met. In less than a minute, the young man tearfully admitted to entering the classroom and, upon finding the teacher's desk unlocked, using his own pen to change his poor grade.

Whether it's a poor grade or a holdup demand note, crooks should realize that forensic technology will have them out.

Documents Experiment #1: Indented Paper
Equipment:
1. Notepad
2. Ballpoint pen
3. Tablespoon of cocoa
4. Cutting board larger than the paper from the notepad
5. Adhesive tape

Write a note on the top page of the notepad (it doesn't hurt if you cheat a little and press just a bit harder than you normally would). Skip lines to help separate words. Tear the page out neatly and set it aside. Tear out the next page and center it on the cutting board. Tape the paper onto the cutting board, being careful not to tape over anywhere the indented writing might be.

Sprinkle the cocoa powder over the page on the cutting board. Carefully pick up the cutting board, keeping it level. Shake the board, again keeping it level, so the powder covers the entire page. As you do this, you should see the letters and words you wrote on the first page appear.

Shake off the excess powder and you should be able to see the entire note (or at least most of it).

If you cannot, you neva' press hard enough on the paper. Come on, no write like a wuss. Press harder and try again.

Documents Experiment #2: Top-of-Letter Analysis
Equipment:
1. Clean, ruled paper
2. Tracing paper
3. Ballpoint pen
4. Ruler or straightedge

Write your name on a line of the ruled paper. Skip three lines, and write your name a second time directly below the first one.

Take the tracing paper and set it on the ruled paper.

On the tracing paper, make a small dot at the highest point of each letter. Using the ruler or straightedge, connect the dots that were made for each name.

You should see a very similar connect-the-dots pattern for each space on the tracing paper where you marked the highest point of the letters of your name.

You can do the same for the bottom-of-letter analysis.

If you don't, why? What you did wrong? They should be similar. What? You wen' try make the two names different? Huh?

9
Injuries and the Autopsy

In too many crimes, people are injured. Unfortunately, in investigations detectives cannot simply depend on the information provided by the ME. We showed this in *Honolulu Homicide* in the case of George Fan, where the Medical Examiner's Office reported there were no injuries on the body. But detectives and crime scene investigators all saw the injuries to Fan's face.

The reality is that no one agency and no one investigator can provide all the answers or make all the decisions in the investigation of a death, for example. Teamwork is the key. But as part of that team, the investigator needs to rise above mediocrity and understand the nature of injuries and the autopsy.

A good investigator will know, by looking at the injury, what type of weapon likely caused the injury. In death cases, investigators should know the classic markers of death. They need to know the difference between a suicidal ligature mark and a homicidal ligature mark. They need to know if the gunshot injury was a contact wound, a close-range wound, or a distant wound. They need to know what hesitation marks are in a stabbing.

It's been said that a good investigator needs to be inquisitive. This is true, but a good investigator needs to be educated as well. For this chapter, we will use the homicide investigation as the focus of discussion and inquiry into injuries, the cause of death, and the autopsy.

Evidence and Injuries

By now you understand that at every crime scene there will be evidence. The investigator must collect all the evidence that can be identified. This evidence will help to bring the facts of the case together. It will help make sense of what happened. It may provide information on the injuries. And the injury evidence may answer questions about a suspicious death.

The Classic Markers of Death

They're called the "classic markers of death" because they have always existed. Rigor mortis and livor mortis can be seen in paintings and sculptures throughout the ages. These classic markers of death can be used to assist the ME to make an estimate on the time when death occurred. Of course, the sooner after death the body is discovered, the easier it will be to determine time of death accurately. In any case, these classic markers of death cannot produce absolutely accurate times of death.

Rigor Mortis

When we die, biochemical changes occur that cause our bodies to stiffen. This condition begins at death, but becomes more noticeable two to four hours after death. Usually, rigor mortis is complete within six to twelve hours and can last for several days, after which it will slowly disappear.

Another form of rigor is the cadaveric spasm. This is known as instantaneous rigor mortis. It can occur suddenly when there is a gunshot injury to the brain, for example. Under regular rigor mortis, it is not possible to simulate a cadaveric spasm by placing a gun, for example, in the hand of a dead person and attempting to have the fingers grip it.

The one example of cadaveric spasm that occurred during my tenure as the lieutenant-in-charge of the Homicide Detail was in a man who, as a result of a prior brain injury, murdered his family, then killed himself. When he was discovered, his hand was firmly gripping the handgun that he used, and the ME pointed it out as a cadaveric spasm.

Livor Mortis

When we die, our heart stops pumping our blood. The blood settles, through the force of gravity, to the lowest point in our bodies. If we are lying on our back, it will settle to our back and the undersides of our arms and legs, for example. This appears as a staining of the skin to a reddish purple or blue color. Livor mortis is also known as postmortem lividity. We first begin to see lividity at about one hour after death, and it reaches full lividity within three to four hours.

Of note, livor mortis does not occur at pressure points when the body is pressed against the floor, for example. This can be observed at the shoulder blades and buttocks of a deceased person lying on his back.

There was an argument years ago between two elderly gentlemen who lived together. It turned into a loud fight, and building security was called. The officer noticed one of the men lying on his side on the living room floor. They agreed to be quiet and the guard went away. Three days later, the guard was called to the same apartment because of a bad odor emanating from it. When he arrived, he found the old man who was lying on the floor was dead.

Upon examination of the body, we could clearly see that the livor mortis was on the side of his body that was facing up, and the side that was resting on the floor had no settling of blood. This contradicted the other man's statement that he found the deceased lying on the floor and did not touch him. With the livor mortis on the upper half of his body, it was clear to us that someone had turned him over. As the other old man was the only other occupant of that apartment, we knew he was lying.

Algor Mortis

Another change when we die is the temperature of our body. Our metabolism stops upon death and our body cools. I like to ask my students, "To what temperature does our body cool when we die?" All kinds of answers come forth—70 degrees, 85 degrees, and so on. The simple answer is that the body cools to the ambient temperature of the surroundings. If indoors, this can be called room temperature. This process usually takes sixteen to twenty-four hours.

Postmortem Changes in the Eyes

Noticeable changes in the eyes occur after death. The corneas dull over and a filmlike covering may appear. This can occur within just a few minutes or up to a few hours, depending on the temperature and humidity and whether the eyelids are open or closed.

Manner of Death

There are four categories that describe the manner of death. There are subcategories that clarify death cases under specific situations, but when the ME makes a decision on the manner of death, it will be recorded in one of these four general categories.

Natural Death

If we die of natural causes, it's called a natural death. And when we die, if our physician signs our death certificate because we were expected to die of natural causes, the classification becomes an "attended death." In this case, our body is released to the private funeral home or mortuary. But if our death was not expected, even though we died of the same natural causes, our physician may choose not to sign our death certificate. In this case, our death is classified as an "unattended death" and our body goes to the ME for a postmortem examination.

Please note that a postmortem examination does not mean that an autopsy will be conducted. With so many cases coming to the attention of the ME, he or she may simply look at the body and, if there are no signs of injury or struggle, conclude that the person died of, for example, "probable arterial sclerotic disease."

Accidental Death

In this category, regardless of what type of accident occurs, if you die under accidental circumstances your death will be classified as "accidental." In my classes on CSI, I ask my students to try to come up with an accident that would not fall into this category. They can't do it—and they never will.

Suicide

Suicide, of course, is the taking of one's own life. It doesn't matter how it's done; the key is that you intentionally cause your own death. A critical issue is whether another person's activity encouraged you to commit suicide. In this case, that person is guilty of manslaughter. The investigation here is important to ensure that the death truly is a suicide and nothing else.

Homicide

It is important to point out that homicide is not defined as murder. Homicide is the taking of a human life by another. In this classification, the death could be further classified into one of several subcategories.

Murder is the first of these subcategories, and in every state there are further subcategories. In Hawai'i, we have murder first-degree and murder second-degree.

Manslaughter is the next subcategory. *Negligent homicide* involves traffic-related deaths. Our penal code also has other subcategories, as in other states. These include *justifiable homicide* and *self-defense.*

Cause of Death

The ME will determine the cause of death. Some people contend that we all die as a result of our heart stopping. Yes, that's true. But *why* does our heart stop? That's the all-important question. Is it from a bullet to the brain? Is it the result of a fall from a penthouse window?

It doesn't matter. What matters is your manner of death. What caused your death can be an endless number of things. How your death is classified among the four manners of death discussed above is the important issue. Let's talk about some injuries and causes of death.

Abrasions

"Daddy, I got a cut!"

"No, sweetheart, you have an abrasion."

Well, my five-year-old doesn't care if what happened to her knee is a cut or an abrasion, a laceration or a contusion. It hurts—so baby her. But in the world of law enforcement, the investigator should know the difference. An abrasion is a scrape of the outer layer of skin, called the epidermis. (I bet you didn't know you were going to get a medical education, huh?) Generally, abrasions do not bleed. And it's important to know that fingernail marks, which can result from a struggle or are found on the back of the neck of a victim who has been strangled, are considered abrasions.

Contusions

Contusions are bruises. These happen when a force is applied to the skin, and bleeding occurs under the skin but has no means to get outside the body. When that happens, you get a bruise. Swelling also usually accompanies contusions.

In rare cases, contusions carry the shape of the weapon delivering the blow. For example, when a semiautomatic handgun is placed up against the skin of a victim and fired, and the slide slams onto the skin as the weapon is fired, the design of the muzzle can, in some cases, be clearly seen in that particular bruise.

Lacerations

These are tears in the skin made by cutting, stabbing, or chopping. (Can't you just hear it? "Daddy, I got a contusion next to the laceration when I fell on the sharp pipe, and I have an abrasion on my other knee that landed on the asphalt." Right.)

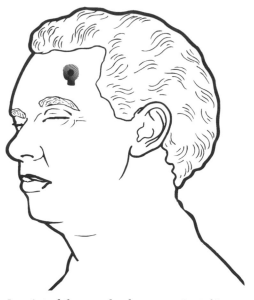

Imprint of the muzzle of a gun against skin

Most lacerations made by cutting have uniform edges where the wound lies at the outer layer of skin. You can see this in razor cuts, for example. In suicide cases, the wound inflicted should correspond with the right- or left-handedness of the victim. A right-handed victim would inflict a suicide laceration wound on the left side and the opposite would be true for a left-handed person. Curiously, however, as you will see in gunshot wounds, a laceration will not give you much information about the weapon, because the injury is so sharp and clean.

Gunshot Wounds

Perhaps the first thing to remember is that a bullet striking a body is traveling at a tremendous rate of speed. It pushes and stretches the skin inward and then tears through. The bullet doesn't just leave a nice clean hole. Around the entry hole there may be a "contusion ring" that occurs when the bullet passes through the stretched skin. In addition to the contusion ring, there may be a "smudge ring" created by debris on the bullet. In many cases, however, this does not occur. A little farther outward from the entry hole you might see an area of tiny frecklelike discoloration—what some people describe as "powder burns." This is the wrong terminology. These are not burns but rather tiny lacerations of the skin made by the impact of unburned gunpowder. A better name for these injuries is *stippling*. Bullet injuries occur in various forms.

Contact Gunshot Wounds

Contact wounds occur when the muzzle of the gun is placed in firm contact with the skin. When the weapon is fired, the gases from the rapidly burning powder follow the bullet into the body. When the contact wound is to the head, some of the gases follow the bullet into the skull, while other gases expand between the skull and the skin, causing the skin to balloon outward. This produces a cruciform, or cross-shaped, tear in the skin. This injury can be seen in nearly all contact gunshot wounds.

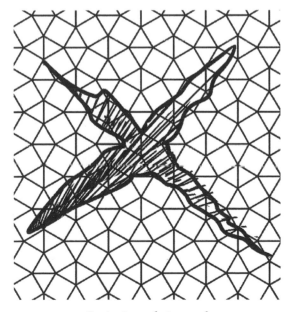

Contact gunshot wound

If the gun's muzzle is not in full contact with the skin, there may not be enough gases to enter under the skin to produce the cruciform-shaped wound. When the muzzle is raised partially on one side at the time the weapon is fired, most of the gas will escape and not enter the victim's body.

The exit gunshot wound usually has no particular shape other than a jagged appearance. The reason for this is that the bullet, traveling in a straight, spinning fashion, has now come into contact with skin and bone. The bullet may flatten or break apart. It may begin to twist and fly wildly out of control after entering the head. If it exits it will shatter and break the bone and skin, and the exit wound will look much different from the entrance wound.

When I was teaching a class of police recruits in the late 1980s, I showed them a slide of a victim who had a contact gunshot wound in the head. The weapon used was a .357 caliber revolver. The entrance wound was clearly visible because the ME had shaved the hair away from the wound. I paused in my description, and out of the darkness came a voice. "Wow! That .357 was so powerful, it even blew the hair away." The class erupted into laughter. I don't know who made the comment, and perhaps it was better that way.

Close Gunshot Wounds

A close gunshot wound—from up to eighteen inches or so— will produce an area that may be soiled with soot and unburned powder. This area will be fairly well defined and readily observable if not stained with the victim's blood. This residue pattern becomes wider and less distinct the farther away from the victim the gun was held when it was fired. Beyond about three feet, this pattern disappears. The entry wound is round, but the exit wound can also be jagged if the bullet is damaged and tumbles after entry.

Distant Gunshot Wounds

We're not talking about hundreds of yards here. Rather, the distant gunshot wound is that which does not have any of the characteristics that were described in the sections on contact and close gunshot wounds. Depending on the model of the weapon, the caliber of the bullet, and the power of the ammunition, a distant gunshot wound can occur as close as eighteen inches.

Stab Wounds

Stab wounds can be made with any pointed object used as a weapon. When a blunt object is used as a stabbing weapon, the wound on the skin may actually be smaller than the diameter of the weapon. This is because of the elasticity of the skin as it is pushed inward. When a cutting weapon is used, the exterior wound may be larger than the weapon's edge because of the cutting action of the weapon.

In many stabbing cases we see defense injuries—cutting or stabbing blows—on the victim's arms and hands, made as the victim tried to deflect the blow or even grab the knife.

Poison

Poison is rarely used as a criminal tool. Usually poison is used as a method of suicide. A person might swallow a caustic acid, for example. Normally there will be a crime scene where investigators will find evidence of the poisoning.

Murder cases usually involve an intimate group or family, and the poison is administered slowly over a period of time.

A common method of suicide is carbon monoxide poisoning. A buildup of carbon monoxide can cause unconsciousness and death within sixty minutes. A person intent on suicide will secure a hose to the exhaust pipe of their car and bring it into the car with them. Slowly, the victims experience numbness in their arms and legs. They become sleepy, lie down, and eventually die. Of course, there are other ways people can be exposed to dangerous amounts of carbon monoxide. A buildup of carbon monoxide can occur in tunnels, shops, and public garages with poor ventilation, and even on heavily used streets on still days.

In some accidental instances of poisoning, the victims died from an overdose of illegal drugs. There was one case in which the body of a young man was found on the living room floor propped up against the sofa. The police received a call from an unknown person who gave the dispatcher the entire story. He and his friend were using heroin at the friend's apartment. They had injected themselves, but his friend wanted more, so he injected himself again. He still wanted more, but the caller said he warned him against doing more because it would overdose him. Nevertheless, his friend injected still again. The caller said he went to the bathroom, and when he came back he found his friend unconscious on the floor with a syringe in his arm, having given himself yet another dose. He tried to wake him, but his friend would not wake up, so he called.

"Why did you leave the scene?" we asked.

He did not wish his identity to be known.

When we arrived, the victim had already been pronounced dead and was going into rigor. In the paramedic's opinion, the man had been dead for several hours.

Apparently, his friend was in no real rush to call for help.

Suffocation

"Suffocation" is a general term for a cause of death that may include a wide variety of methods. For example, "The cause of death is suffocation due to ligature strangulation," or "The cause of death is suffocation due to crushing force to the chest."

In suffocation deaths, petechial hemorrhaging will occur in many cases. This appears as tiny, sometimes pinpoint ruptures and blood clots of the surface blood vessels in the face, neck, and eyes resulting from the great pressure associated with suffocation and strangulation.

Crushing Injuries

Once, when I was a young boy, a construction company was putting a sewer line in our street. One day there was a great commotion, and I eventually learned that a man was killed because the side of the trench caved in and buried him. His coworkers were able to free his head so that he could get air, but he still could not breathe. He soon died, his chest crushed by the rock and dirt that pressed in on him. Although I never saw him myself, the event has stuck with me.

Drowning

In Hawai'i we must ensure that we "waterproof" our children and teach them how to be safe in the water. "Drowning" is the term applied to the blocking of the lungs by a liquid. This can be water, mud, or any other liquid substance that can be inhaled.

In most drowning cases, the victim is found floating face down with the lower back raised. Early in my career with the Homicide Detail, we had a drowning case on the Windward coast. When the man was pulled from the water by the Honolulu Fire Department rescue team, he had injuries to his face, head, hands, and feet. It was puzzling until the ME explained that while he was floating in the shallow water, those parts of the body had been injured by being dragged over the rocks by the motion of the waves.

Strangulation

Victims can be strangled by a ligature or by hand. Strangulation by ligature usually leaves a furrow where the cord or ligature went around the neck. If the murder was committed by hand, there will be bruising on the front of the neck and fingernail marks on the back of the neck. In either case, the halting of air to the lungs, not the blockage of the arteries, is usually the cause of death.

In these cases, there should be signs of a struggle and other violence, so the investigators should be aware of any other related injuries.

Hanging

In hanging cases, the ligature stops the air to the lungs, but unlike strangulation, it also stops the flow of blood to the brain. Hanging is

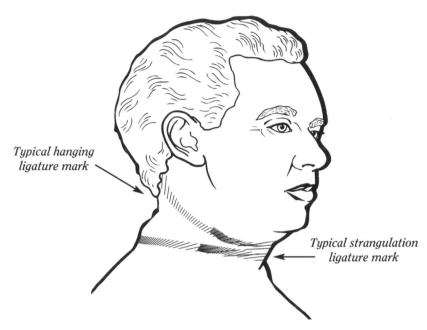

*Typical hanging
ligature mark*

*Typical strangulation
ligature mark*

Ligature differences in hanging versus murder by strangulation

accomplished by the weight of the body tightening the ligature. Unconsciousness occurs rather quickly, and death soon follows.

In hanging cases, the ligature mark is found high on the neck, slanted backward and upward toward the back of the head.

In ligature strangulation cases, the ligature groove and bruising are usually found lower on the neck and parallel to the shoulders, rather than moving in an upward pattern to the base of the skull.

Murder by hanging is a rare occurrence. But in both types of cases, if a ligature is used and in place when the body is found, the knot must be preserved. It should be removed by cutting the ligature away from the knot so it may be examined later.

Suffocating

This occurs when there is blockage to the nose and mouth, which may result from a soft object being pressed against them. In some cases involving babies and older persons, there may be no indication of suffocation or any other injuries.

There was a case in which an older woman was found dead in her bed. Because of the persistence of a beat officer who "just had a feeling," an autopsy was performed and it was determined that the woman was raped and murdered. It was a case that might have been completely overlooked because of her age and the fact that she had no other injuries. Remember that a postmortem examination can simply be a viewing of the body. Her death might have been closed out as "probable arterial sclerotic disease."

Another type of death that is sometimes overlooked is the death of an infant in a Munchausen syndrome by proxy case. These cases occur when a woman looks for sympathy by injuring her baby, usually by blocking the air from entering the nose and mouth.

In all instances of suffocation, the investigator must be keenly aware of finding other items of evidence.

Electric Shock

This is a rare cause of death, and it is usually found in accidents. When electric current passes through the body, there will be entry and exit points that have burn marks, and clothing may also be burned.

In the course of my six years with the Homicide Detail, there were only two deaths by electric current to which we responded. One was a woman who was electrocuted when she leaned over her washing machine, which had shorted out in the rain. The other was a repairman who touched a live wire on a utility pole. Both cases were ruled to be accidents.

The Role of the Entomologist

There are times in the course of investigating a death case that the expertise of an entomologist is required. We are honored in Hawai'i to have one of the best. Dr. Lee Goff, who established a forensic entomology specialty at the University of Hawai'i, is now at Chaminade University of Honolulu. He has been to many, many death crime scenes.

Entomologists provide assistance in determining when the victim died by studying the insect life on, in, and around the body. When called to a crime scene, the entomologist recovers live insects and flies, their pupae, their larvae, and their maggots from the body and the surrounding area. These are taken back to the lab and a life cycle of the recovered specimens is produced. Studying this life cycle, the entomologist can estimate very accurately the length of time since the victim died.

Flies are attracted to a body very quickly after death. They lay their eggs on the body and their life cycle begins. Dr. Goff's examinations have provided our Homicide Detail with information that we were able to use to support confessions or disprove alibis. The case of Pauline Rodriguez, described in *Honolulu Homicide,* is one example of Dr. Goff's work, proving crucial to solving the murder.

The Autopsy

As mentioned earlier, the autopsy is a postmortem examination whereby the pathologist examines the body in great detail by studying the injuries, the external body, and the internal organs.

When the body arrives at the morgue, it should be weighed and measured for height. The clothing should be removed very carefully and properly preserved.

Both the clothed body and the disrobed body should be photographed. Every stage of the autopsy should also be photographed to document and preserve a record of that particular aspect of the investigation. Garments should be recovered separately, and blood-stained clothing should be allowed to dry.

When the body is clothed and when it is disrobed, it should be searched for any trace evidence. Fingerprints should be taken from the body. This is done in much the same manner as it would be if the person were being fingerprinted in a police station, except there would be no cooperation. Ink is applied to the fingers, and the technician rolls the fingers onto a card. The prints are labeled and recovered into evidence.

Very briefly, and without making any claim to expertise, I offer the following general description of the autopsy in layman terms. This description comes from observing multiple autopsies in the course of my career, and I offer my apologies for any errors in terminology, sequence, or procedure. As with mathematics, I make no claim to having in-depth knowledge of this medical procedure. So I am reporting only what my eyes have seen.

The body is opened by incising a V pattern from the shoulders to the sternum and from the sternum to the pubic area. The skin, the layer of fat, and the layer of muscle are examined and pulled back, exposing the inner organs. In gunshot and stabbing cases, slender metal rods are inserted into the wounds to illustrate the trajectory or path the weapon took before these incisions were made. These trajectory patterns will enable the pathologist to determine not only the trajectory but also which internal organs may have been injured by the weapon.

The incisions complete, the pathologist begins to examine each of the internal organs, describing the condition of each. The major organs are removed and weighed and a sample taken for later laboratory and toxicological examination. During this process, the pathologist searches for any weapons or instruments that may have been left inside the body—bullets and broken knife tips, for example. Also, during the entire course of this procedure, the pathologist is recording the autopsy via audio recorder and photographing those areas of importance to the investigation and examination.

In cases where the injury is located somewhere other than the torso of the body—a leg, for example—the pathologist will incise that wound to determine size and depth. If it's a shooting, he will recover any bullet remaining in the wound.

When all organs have been removed and weighed and samples are collected, they are placed in plastic bags and set aside to be replaced in the body later.

The throat is examined for any injury, as strangling or suffocation injuries may not be readily apparent.

The brain is also examined. To access the brain, incisions are made across the top of the head from ear to ear, and the skin flap is pulled back toward the face. The skull is cut in a wedgelike pattern using a medical saw and the piece removed, exposing the brain. The brain, an organ itself, is removed and weighed and a sample taken as with the others.

One of the duties of the pathologist is to determine if there was any cause of death other than the ones we may think obvious. Pathologists also look for signs of disease, and indeed, in noncriminal-related autopsies, that is precisely what they are looking for.

The autopsy is over. The organs are put back into the body cavity, the torso and other incisions are sewn together, and the body is placed into a bag for storage until it is released to a mortuary.

In criminal cases, the autopsy report and the accompanying audio tapes and photographs are evidence that can be used later in court.

A Final Word

Teamwork is an important factor in the investigation of suspicious deaths or murders. Each agency—the police, the ME, and the prosecuting attorney—has a specific role to play in this objective. No one agency can do without the other. The goal is to find, prosecute, and convict the killer. We owe this to the victim and to the victim's family.

Injuries and the Autopsy Experiment #1: To da Bone

Note: This experiment can get you in trouble with your neighbors and the Department of Health. Proceed at your own risk.

Equipment:

1. A quarter-inch wood-frame-and-wire-mesh cage (handmade by you) eighteen inches square
2. Five-pound pork butt with bone
3. Camera and film

Build the mesh cage. Make the wooden frame in whatever fashion you wish, and attach the mesh to ensure only flies and small insects can enter. Make the top side separate so you can remove and/or secure it to the cage.

Place the cage outside as far away from your bedroom window as possible.

Thaw the pork butt to room temperature. Take it to the cage and place it inside. Ensure that the cage lid is secure so wild animals or wild neighbors cannot open it. Take a picture of the pork butt on day one. Allow the pork butt to sit undisturbed. Every day, at approximately the same time, take another picture of the pork butt. Do not disturb the cage.

Record how many days it takes for the flies, maggots, and insect life to devour the pork butt to the bone.

Record how many days it takes your neighbors to call the police.

10
Graphic Art

There is a little-known area of forensic science that the public does not often see: graphic art. Some may argue that graphic art is not a science. Perhaps in the strictest sense, that's true. But while not a scientific discipline such as chemistry and biology, graphic art can be equally important. Graphic artists of the police agencies across the nation are involved in myriad tasks, from preparing posters for noncriminal issues to reconstructing the facial features of unidentified skeletal remains.

In the course of my tour of duty with the Homicide Detail, the Honolulu Police Department's graphic artists—Joseph Aragon and Chun Yee, the illustrators of this book—were called upon time and again to create composite drawings of possible suspects. These drawings are generated from the descriptions of witnesses who may have seen a suspect running from a crime scene.

Composite Drawings

Composite drawings are perhaps the most common criminal work graphic artists perform. In many police departments, a computer program is used to prepare composite drawings. When the drawing is completed, of course, it looks like a computer drawing. The artists for the Honolulu Police Department, however, create the drawing freehand. This work requires a lot of patience in their interaction with the witnesses. They must get the witness to recall what they saw—feature by feature. And these features can be numerous, as the following list indicates.

- *The shape of the head:* People have differently shaped heads—round, oval, or long, for example.

- *The height of the forehead in relation to the eyebrows:* Some people have very little distance from their eyebrows to their hair line. Others have foreheads that go from their eyebrows to the back of their head. I've noticed my forehead has been growing as I've aged. I've heard people say it's a sign of maturity. That's a better description than the term "balding."
- *The hair:* People wear their hair in very specific styles. Was the hair long (lower than the shoulder), shoulder length, neck length, short, covering the ears? The artist must be able to demonstrate the difference between neck length and shoulder length, for example. Was the hair curly, straight, wavy, or kinky (with very tight curls)? Was the hair dark, light, gray, white? A good artist can represent, through shading, the color of the hair.
- *The neck:* Necks are long and slender, short and squat—or did it appear that the suspect's head was sitting directly on his shoulders?
- *The eyes:* Eyes often differ according to our race. Eyes can be oval, elongated, round, close together, far apart. What about the eyebrows? They can be thick, thin, arched, peaked, or straight across. Does the eyebrow run from one eye to the other?
- *Ears:* Are there loose lobes or are the lobes attached to the cheek? If they are loose, are they big and floppy? Remember that old childhood song, "Do your ears hang low, do they wobble to and fro, can you tie them in a knot, can you tie them in a bow?" (Did I just put a song in your head that you can't get rid of?)
- *The nose:* Oh, don't we all have different shapes to our noses! They range from a small wee bump on the face to Jimmy Durante's schnoz. Some people don't like the look of their nose so they have it adjusted, shaped, and reconditioned for lots and lots of money. I say it's cheaper to just step into the ring with a professional fighter. Your nose will soon have a different

shape. One aspect of the nose that we completely overlook is the nostrils. Is the nose upturned, allowing the nostrils to look like black holes in the face, or does the nose bend downward so you cannot see the nostrils at all? Was there nostril hair? Don't laugh. Some people have bushes coming from their nostrils. It could be a distinguishing feature that might help capture the suspect. Another very important feature is the distance from the nose to the lips: Was it wide, medium, or small?

- *Glasses:* Were there glasses resting on that nose? If so, did they have clear lenses or tinted—what color? What did the frames look like? Were they thin wire in the current fashion or the black plastic frames from our childhood days?

- *Facial hair:* Did he have a moustache? Did *she* have a moustache? What shape was the moustache? Was it big and bushy or was it like the Moustachio Petes of mafia fame? What about the cheeks? Was he unshaven? Did he have a beard, and what shape was it? Unfortunately, some people have facial hair running all the way down their neck to their shoulder. Others have chest hair curling up from their shirt to their chin.

- *Speaking of the chin:* Some people have large, protruding chins and jaws. Others have what can be described as weak chins—those that are recessed or small in relation to the rest of their head. Others' necks begin at the end of their chin. As we get older, we develop loose skin just under our chin. This is normal in the aging process—except for those same people who don't like their noses. That extra skin is clipped away, also for lots and lots of money. (Save yourself the cash and just put a rubber band stretching from the top of your head to where your neck and chin meet.) Was there a cleft in the chin or any other distinguishing feature?

- *Race:* What race (or ethnicity) was the suspect? We need to be careful here. Some people object to the different terms we use, whether we're describing race, ethnicity, or nationality. One elderly gentleman threatened to sue me because I described a suspect once in a TV interview. I called him Portuguese. The poor guy went berserk. "He's not Portuguese, he's Caucasian. I'm calling my attorney!" I replied, "But he was Portuguese. I can tell. I am one myself." I didn't win the argument. The same applies to Hawaiian, Samoan, Tongan, and so forth. Some people object to these distinctions. They are Polynesian. The bottom line is, we're all human—except for a couple of guys I know.

- *Tattoos:* Did this suspect have any noticeable tattoos? Where were they on his body? What color or colors were they? What was the tattoo? We rarely see the tattoo "Mom" anymore. Today, you're likely to see something obscene. If the suspect was a woman, don't immediately assume she does not have a tattoo. I have never been tattooed myself (the damn thing hurts and I don't like needles!).

- *Height and weight:* This is a difficult issue because people have different opinions of how tall or how heavy a person is. But give it a shot, anyway.

- *The body shape:* This can be skinny, large, or muscular. There are a million descriptions, because we're all different.

- *Clothes:* Did the suspect have on clothing? Many years ago, the culprit in a bank robbery put a packet of money down the front of his pants. Little did he know that the packet was an exploding dye pack. Dye packs look like a pack of real money. But when they pass by the electronic eye at the exit to the bank, they explode some seconds later. This poor crook had it go off right next to the family jewels. It caught his underwear on fire and for a little while, money was the least of his concerns. He yanked off his pants, ripped off his underwear, and slapped himself silly trying to put out the fire between his legs. When he finally extinguished the flames, he realized that his underwear and pants were reduced to a pile of smoldering ash. So he took off down the street. When we asked witnesses what he looked like, the responses we had were mostly, "I didn't see his face, but I can tell you all about his . . ." We did catch him, by the way—at The Queen's Medical Center emergency room!

You would be surprised to learn just how much you can remember about a suspect after having seen him for only a few seconds—clothed or not. These composite drawings have been, from case to case, very successful in identifying crooks. People see the drawings and say, "Hey, that's Joe Crook."

Facial Reconstruction

On a few occasions we ask the graphic artist to go to the morgue to look at the face of a dead person who has no identification and no fingerprints on file (determined by running the prints through our Automated Fingerprint Identification System). The artist will try to draw a portrait of the deceased as closely as possible as he or she would look in life. The finished drawing is published in the print and TV media in an attempt to find anyone who might know who he or she was.

Then there is another type of facial reconstruction—that of skeletal remains. This is a difficult and tedious process. The artists must be trained, as both Aragon and Yee have been. They learn that anthropologists have conducted studies of the various races and learned that there are skeletal differences. The differences lie in the shape of our skulls, in the eye orbits, and in the nose openings. Then they conduct studies as to the depth of tissue from skin to bone. These distances vary at different locations on our skulls.

The facial reconstruction requires the artist, using these measurements of depth from skin to bone, to glue rubber rods (that look very similar to pencil erasers) at the various locations cited in the studies. The artist then applies modeling clay to the skull, bringing the clay up to the level of the rubber rods. By smoothing the clay and adding medium features such as ears, eyebrows, and hair, they come up with a bust of the deceased.

This bust can then be used in broadcast media to help identify the remains. Instead of using the actual skull, however, a casting is usually made and the victim's skull is returned to the ME.

A Final Word

The Honolulu Police Department should be very proud of the quality work performed by its graphic artists. The work that Chun and Joe have done will be difficult to replicate when they retire. And I'm not saying this just because they drew the illustrations in this book.

11
Forensic Profiling

One of the most valuable tools in the investigation of serial killing cases is forensic profiling. Serial killings, the murders committed by a stranger against a stranger, are the most difficult murders to investigate. After the murder, the killer may move on to another district or another state. Or as in the Green River serial killings in the state of Washington, the killer may remain unknown for many years simply because of the stranger-to-stranger relationship between killer and victims.

As a serial killer is frightening to the community, he is equally challenging to the police investigating his murders. He could be anyone. In the late 1970s and early 1980s, the FBI established a new unit that assisted police in the investigation of serial killings and major murder cases. The unit was headed by Agents John Douglas and Robert Ressler, who brought personality profiling into the picture as an investigative tool.

Profiling is not magic. It is rather the systematic study of the crime scene. It's the understanding of the background of most serial killers. It's an understanding of the minds of serial killers. And it's the reality-based forecast of what kind of person that serial killer might be. To better understand forensic profiling of a serial killer, it is important to understand some of the key processes and situations that a person may experience that may cause him to develop into a serial killer.

It is also necessary to understand the definition of a sexual murder. As defined by the FBI, sexual murder is *"an act of control, dominance, and performance that is representative of an underlying fantasy embedded with violence, sexuality, and death."*

Motivational Model

In 1986 Douglas and Ressler, along with Ann Burgess, Carol Hartman, and Arlene McCormack, published a motivational model in the *Journal of Interpersonal Violence*. In this article, they discuss the patterns of social interaction that serial killers have acknowledged they go through as they grow up. It should be noted up front that many people, poor or not, have had a childhood just like that of a serial killer, but they do not grow up to become one. There lies the crucial question. Why does one become a killer and not the others?

As young children, the serial killers-to-be experience an ineffective social environment. They have parents or guardians who ignore their behavior. These adults are nonsupporting and nonprotective. In the eyes of society, these adults are deviants. The children experience abuse, both physical and sexual, at the hands of the people who are supposed to be their caregivers.

As the child grows, these childhood experiences evolve. Patterns arise. The now deviant youth grows more and more isolated. He becomes rebellious and aggressive. He lies, prefers autoerotic behavior to normal sexual activity, and feels a sense of entitlement. This entitlement is not expressed as "society owes me a living," as it is in many people. Rather, it is expressed as "I can do anything I want to."

The adolescent begins to develop cognitive behavior that he knows is wrong, but he does it anyway. He has daydreams and fantasies wrought with strong, deviant sexual thoughts. Themes arise: dominance, violence, power and control, torture and death. Sometimes he will light fires, other times he will torture or kill animals.

This deviant young adult begins to act out his deviant thoughts. He may assault people, commit rape, and even commit nonsexual murder. He is cruel.

More frightening, he begins to justify his actions.

The Role of Fantasy

This serial killer-to-be uses his fantasies as a blueprint for what he does and how he does it. He recognizes his errors and corrects them. He knows he is doing wrong, rationalizes his actions, and plans not to get caught. His fantasies grow and become more elaborate. He uses his fantasies to build on his dominance and power and control. He satisfies his deviance through his isolated erotic activities.

Then one day, he is no longer satisfied with his evil and erotic fantasies alone, so he goes out and finds a victim. His fantasies come to life, and he begins his dark journey as a serial killer.

What Does a Serial Killer Look Like?

Most serial killers look just like normal people. Some of them are good looking. Ted Bundy, for example, was handsome and could be charming. Inwardly, these killers feel alone and powerless. But they become all-powerful and have feelings of complete control and dominance when they take a victim. Ted Bundy once said to his captor that no greater power could a man have than over the life and death of someone else.

Serial killers are mostly men—white men. Serial killers of other races are rare, and female serial killers are just as rare.

These people often are fascinated with forensic science and police work. After all, they don't want to get caught. They are night people. They're loners. And they're constantly looking for their next victim.

The FBI has noted that serial killers often kill within their own race and stick to specific patterns. Bundy's victim "type" was Caucasian brunettes with long hair parted in the middle.

These killers like to kill with their hands—to beat and bludgeon and strangle. If they are not stopped, the pace of murders will accelerate because the killer always needs another victim.

At a seminar I attended in New York, various psychiatrists said that these people are not psychotic. They know what they are doing. They try to avoid capture. Rather, these people have personality disorders and they're antisocial.

And finally, psychiatrists and the FBI agree that serial killers cannot be rehabilitated. They believe that these people will kill until they die themselves or go to prison. Many serial killers have told FBI researchers that if released from prison, they would kill again—and again, and again.

Organized vs. Disorganized

The FBI profilers use crime scene characteristics to help them come to a decision as to the type of serial killer at work. And yes, there are several types: *organized* killers, *disorganized* killers, or a combination of both. Ted Bundy is said to have "devolved" from an organized killer to a disorganized killer as his string of murders increased. The table below illustrates just a few of the differences in the crime scene characteristics of organized and disorganized serial killers. You may recognize that many of the characteristics of organized killers are the mirror opposite of disorganized killers.

Sadly, these characteristics have been developed by examination of the many, many murders committed by sexual and serial killers, most of whose victims have been women and children. Even more sadly, to obtain more information about the killers, more murders must occur for the investigators and profilers to study.

Crime Scene Characteristics of Serial Killers

Organized Serial Killer	Disorganized Serial Killer
The victim was a targeted stranger	The victim was a spontaneous stranger
The crime scene resonates control	The crime scene is messy and disorderly
Restraints may be used	No restraints are used
Sexual acts may occur before the killing	Sexual acts may occur after the killing
The victim's body may be hidden	The victim's body may be left in the open

The crime scene characteristics, the motivational model, and personality attributes give way to an individual profile construction of organized and disorganized killers. The table below provides you with just a few characteristics. As with the crime scene characteristics, the profiles reveal the opposite natures of these two types of people.

Individual Profile Construction of Serial Killers

Organized Serial Killer	Disorganized Serial Killer
Average to above-average intelligence	Below-average intelligence
Socially competent	Socially inadequate
Sexually competent	Sexually incompetent
Living with a partner	Living alone
Controlled emotion during the killing	High anxiety during the killing

The organized or disorganized traits are clues to the type of person the serial killer is and can give investigators important clues to the person they're seeking. These clues can also describe what happens before, during, and after a sexual murder.

The Stages of a Sexual Murder

Through their studies, the FBI has identified stages that occur in a sexual or serial murder.

Stage 1

The first phase of this type of murder is the preparation for the selection of a victim. The killer will go over the fantasy in his mind again and again, refining it and practicing the actions in his head. He may attempt to avoid killing in some cases, but his drive is too great and he gives in to his craving for power, dominance, and death.

Sexual or serial killers can be triggered into action by their fantasy, which is their plan or blueprint, or by some environmental cue—a condition or event that causes the killer to invoke his fantasy.

Stage 2

In this stage, the killer begins the process of the murder. He must first select a victim. In doing this, the organized and the disorganized killer will proceed differently

The organized killer will plan his action in line with his fantasy. A scenario may be that the organized killer will go to a bar, sit down and order a drink, and pretend to watch the football game on the big-screen TV. While he wants to be alone as he sits in the bar, he is searching the crowd for a potential victim. If he selects one, then all his actions will be sharply focused on "obtaining" her. He may do a number of things. He may ask to sit with her, buy her a drink perhaps. He may be friendly and walk her to her car because it's late and dark outside. Or he may simply wait for her to come outside and abduct her before she can get into her car. But in many instances, as reported by serial killers themselves, once he has focused on her, there is little she can do to escape him.

The disorganized killer, on the other hand, may go to the same bar, sit down and order a drink, and watch the football game. That's why he went to the bar—for the alcohol, the game, and to be alone in the corner where he sits. He doesn't want company; he's busy with the game and his booze. When the game is over, he pays his bill and goes back outside to his vehicle, which is usually an older model car. He drives off. Then perhaps he sees a woman hitchhiking along the roadway. A hitchhiking woman is his environmental cue. It triggers his fantasy into action and from that moment on, all of his efforts will be designed to obtain his victim and complete his fantasy. As with the organized killer, when the disorganized killer is triggered into action, there is little that his intended victim can do to escape him.

In each instance the selection of the victim is vastly different, but when it is made, the odds that she will soon be murdered are great.

A very big problem arises for the killer who initially gives in to his fantasy and attempts to kill his first victim: She fights back. This probably is not a part of his fantasy. He wants control. He wants dominance. He wants to be powerful over her. Why is she fighting back? That's not what he planned.

In my investigation classes, I jokingly ask if anyone wants extra credit. Invariably, hands go up. I select one male and tell him, "For ten points extra credit, kill her," and I point to a woman who also had her hand up. I then ask her, "Are you just going to sit there and let him kill you?" She says no. And what would she do to prevent him from killing her? Oh, there are so many things she would do: scream, punch, kick, grab his genitals, bite him, poke his eyes. By now the class is laughing. But in real life, that killer experiences the same from his victim. He may have to fight harder, he becomes out of breath, he may be injured. But he somehow manages to kill her. But something's wrong. He didn't experience the great pleasure he expected from his act. So he needs to do something. "What is it?" I ask the class.

He needs to alter and refine his fantasy. He needs to gain better control of his victim. He perhaps needs to use restraints. He perhaps needs to knock her unconscious before gaining control of her. Bundy acknowledged that in some cases, he would strike his victim on the head with a heavy metal object, sometimes a tire iron, rendering her unconscious before binding her. In other words, the killer has used feedback from his killing to make his fantasy better. It's called a "feedback filter." We all do this—in our jobs, in our relationships. We use experience to improve our actions.

Stage 3

He has committed the murder. His fantasy has peaked. But it's not over yet. What is he going to do with the body? This stage must have been thought of in his fantasy. If not, there is a big confrontation with reality. There in front of him lies a dead woman. What is he going to do? If he has not already developed a plan, he will for the next time. He alters his fantasy again to include the disposal of the body.

Many things can happen here. He could decide to simply leave her where she lies. He could choose to transport her to a location where she may not be found. He may want to display her in an offensive manner. Whatever he does, it also needs to be part of that heinous fantasy.

Stage 4

Here, the killer has experienced his fantasy. He has made observations on how to improve his fantasy, how to better gain control and power over his victim. He has thought of new ways to avoid getting caught by the police.

But there is one more thing: The body must be found. It must be discovered. This insecure man has just committed the most awful act; he has just sinned the ultimate sin. He has just shown that woman how powerful he is. And he doesn't want that excitement to end. He wants more power. He wants power over the community— power over all the people who know he is out there stalking them. He wants them to fear him.

For this to happen, the victim must be found. The community must know what he did. In most cases, where he puts her will result in someone finding her. But what happens if no one finds her? How does he extend his power? She must be found! It's the culmination of his fantasy, the fantasy that drives him on and on. So he calls the police and gives them clues. Or he writes to the newspaper and tells them where she is.

In some rare cases, the fantasy that she must be found is so great that he actually turns himself in to the police. He becomes so self-centered that even his apprehension is overcome by his feeling of power. "Look at me! Look at what I did!" he says.

The Profiling Process

It's not magic. With detailed information from the crime scene, people experienced in putting the clues together can develop a personality profile of the killer.

The first step is getting all the crime scene information. The FBI calls this information *profiling inputs*. These are obtained through the police reports, crime scene investigative reports, photography, and diagrams. They need the pathological information that tells them the cause of death, the wounds suffered, whether there were pre- or postmortem sexual acts, autopsy reports, and photos. Included in these profiling inputs is *victimology*.

"Victimology" describes the collection of a detailed portrait of the victim. More than just height and weight, hair color, eye color, and age, the profiling team wants information on the victim's habits. They want her family structure. They want to know where she worked and how she got there. Who were her friends? Did she have any enemies and why? Was there any drug use? Everything you can think of, they want to know. This information will help them to know the victim and perhaps why she was selected by the killer to be his ultimate horrifying prize.

All of this information is gathered and studied and a decision model is made in step two. The profilers come up with what may have been the intent of the killer. They determine victim risk and offender risk, and they try to determine where in the series of murders her death falls and whether the killings are escalating.

Victim and offender risk seem to correlate inversely. If the victim was a woman who worked in a busy place, wore conservative clothing, tried to never walk alone or be in unsafe places, then her victim risk was very low. On the other hand, if she hitchhiked along dark roadways, went to bars alone, used illegal drugs, or was a prostitute, her victim risk was very high. If the killer made an attempt to abduct the victim from the middle of a crowded shopping mall parking lot at two o'clock in the afternoon on Christmas Eve, his offender risk was extremely high. If he picked up a young prostitute hitchhiking on a dark, lonely street, his offender risk was very low.

With these decisions made, the profilers move to step three and make a crime assessment. They determine whether the killer was organized or disorganized. They decide whether the crime was staged and what motivation the killer may have had. They assess the crime scene dynamics and then reconstruct the crime.

In step four, they conduct the profile. They suggest physical characteristics of the killer in line with his organized or disorganized status. What kind of habits would a person like this have? What kind of demographics are probable under these conditions? And they make recommendations to the investigators.

With this done, the investigative team may be able to find leads that point to a particular suspect. More likely, they must wait for yet another murder to occur. Then the entire process begins again with the new evidence from the recent case. This will continue until the killer is caught or leaves their jurisdiction—or dies.

A Final Word

Forensic profiling is not rocket science, but it's not child's play either. It is tedious. It involves a dedicated effort to look at all the evidence and make correct decisions regarding the suspect's possible personality. The word "possible" is important, because this killer may be different than the studies have suggested. But different or not, the effort must be a dedicated one. Because after all, someone's child has been murdered.

Forensic Profiling Experiment #1: Who Am I Describing?

Take the time to sit down and write down all of your own personality traits and characteristics that you can think of. Stay away from concrete items such as weight and color of eyes and hair and gender. Focus instead on "who you are." Most important, *be honest* with yourself. Following are some of the questions you can ask yourself in order to list traits:

- Am I kind most of the time? Or is there a streak of ornery in me?
- Do I smile, am I noncommittal, or do I frown a lot?
- Do I get excited in a good way when people are happy, or do I get excited in a bad way because someone made a mistake?
- Do I like children, or do I prefer them at a distance, say in someone else's house?
- How do I answer the telephone?
- Do people come to me at work and talk good naturedly, or do they prefer to leave me to myself?

You can see the trend of the questions. List the good and bad points in a way that will not give you away. For example:

- This person rarely smiles.
- This person prefers adults to children.

At the bottom of your list write this:

Personality Types
Dictator	Friendly
Businessman	Show-off

Make several copies of your list and give them to people you know—family, friends, coworkers. Tell them it's an experiment from Harvard University; it will make them think you're more important than they ever figured, and they'll complete the test.

Provide them with a stamped envelope addressed to you. Ask them to read the characteristics, think about what type of person those characteristics would describe, and then circle only one of the personality types listed above. Tell them not to put their name on the paper. It should be completely anonymous. We don't want you scratching them off your Christmas list.

Next, instruct them to put it in the envelope and mail it back to you.

You may be surprised at the type of person your family, friends, and coworkers think those traits suggest.

Yup, that's you—all those different types of personalities that your friends and family said you were through the survey. Each of us has many sides to us: happy, sour, mean, joyful. People sometimes see us very differently. Understanding this can be important, especially if most of the people circle "dictator" while you thought you were "friendly."

12
Crime Scene Tools

Have you ever watched a TV show on CSI where the technician walks in with that small briefcase and gets the entire scene processed with the tools from that little Eddie Bauer bag? Hold on one second. That's not his crime scene tools—that's his lunch!

The crime scene tools needed to process any major crime scene are kept in a panel truck or van. Don't let that TV show fool you into thinking that processing a crime scene is easy. I remember watching one show where they arrived at the scene and seven minutes later the overpaid lead guy tells the rest of them, "Okay, boys, we're done here." Then he flashes his gleaming teeth at the camera and makes way for a commercial. Let me give you an idea how it really is. Think sweat. Think sore back. Try to remember when you last ate something. "Got any aspirin?" "Wait, my eyes hurt, I need a break."

Investigating a crime scene in real life is not all that picture-perfect, made-for-TV pretend stuff you see on the tube. It's tedious, sometimes difficult work that requires a technician with more grit than gleaming teeth, a technician who knows what to do—and what to do first—and which process could destroy potential evidence. That technician will also have all of his or her tools, equipment, and materials at hand.

"Excuse me, Lieutenant, I need to go to Longs to pick up some masking tape. Everybody take a smoke break—I'll be back. Anybody need anything?" This is a really quick way to make an enemy of the lieutenant.

Equipment

The proper crime scene equipment does not fit into one bag.

Investigators truly need a vehicle that can hold the items needed to properly process the crime scene. Let's look at some of the items in the evidence technician's van.

Photographic Equipment
- 35 mm camera
- 1:1 camera
- digital camera (optional)
- tripod(s)
- film (both color and black and white)
- flash unit(s)
- batteries (fresh ones)
- rulers to show scale

If you're a camera buff (I'm not) I'll wager you can think of additional items for the technician to bring.

Diagram Equipment
- graph paper
- unlined paper
- sharpened pencils
- erasers
- clipboards
- 50' tape measure

What else can you think of to bring in order to create a draft diagram at a crime scene?

Latent Fingerprint Equipment
- nylon fingerprint brushes
- magna-brushes
- fingerprint lifting tape (lots)
- black carbon fingerprint powder
- fluorescent fingerprint powders
- colored fingerprint powders
- 3" x 5" preprinted fingerprint cards

- portable laser unit
- magnifying glass
- heavy-duty flashlight
- extra-bright lights
Anything else?

Blood Equipment
- envelopes (for dried blood)
- vials (for wet blood)
- luminol reagent
- phenolphthalein
- clean spray bottles
- cotton swabs
- Q-tip swabs
- saline
- plastic pipettes (to recover wet blood)

Every crime scene technician can add to my list.

Impression Recovery Equipment
- photo equipment listed above
- dental stone powder
- plaster-of-paris powder
- wooden frames of various sizes (for dams)
- silicone rubber
- empty five-gallon paint buckets (to mix the powders)
- five gallons of water (there may be no other water source to mix powders)

I definitely feel like I'm leaving something out.

Tools
- hammers
- screwdrivers

- wrenches
- socket wrenches
- power drills
- drill bit kit
- pliers (all kinds and sizes)
- bolt cutters
- wire cutters
- handsaws (all kinds and sizes)
- hacksaw and extra blades
- electric rotary saws
- power drills
- shovels
- metal cold chisels
- pry bars (all sizes)
- wood chisels
- electrical extension cords

General and Miscellaneous Equipment
- latex gloves
- magnets
- chalk
- paper bags
- plastic bags
- scissors
- evidence tags
- ladders
- portable vacuum cleaner
- vacuum cleaner filters
- metal detector
- portable generator
- stand-up lights (regular and flood)
- heavy gloves
- cotton gloves
- towels

• drinking water
• cups
• umbrellas
• safety cones
• rope (25')
• chain (8')

A Final Word

This list is not complete, I'm sure. Nor will it fit into that smiling TV technician's leather bag that looks like it never touched a dirty surface.

Oops, I'm forgetting one thing: peanut butter and jelly sandwiches—or Zippy's chili coupons. Don't forget the extra rice and macaroni salad, with kimchi on the side. Remember, you still get hungry.

Bonus Section

Protect Yourself in a Dangerous World

13
Prevention

Open any Hawai'i newspaper, on any island, on any day of the year. You won't need to search long to find articles of someone in Hawai'i who was a victim of a crime. You'll find stories of people who have been victims of property crimes or of violent crimes against a person.

"It doesn't happen in Hawai'i," goes a phrase from bygone days. Anyone living in the real world no longer believes this. So what does happen in Hawai'i? What happens in Honolulu? Property crime happens—at one of the highest rates in the nation. Rape happens. Serial killing happens. Mass murder happens. Drug abuse happens.

Does anyone need examples? About property crimes, ask a neighbor. Odds are that one of your neighbors has been a victim of a property crime sometime during the past year. Sexual offenses occur in Hawai'i at a frightening rate, more frequently than we would like to believe. Sexual serial murders have entered our city as well. In 1986 five young Honolulu women were raped and strangled. In 1988 Orlando Ganal murdered five people in a jealous rage. In 1999 people across the nation read about a mass murder in the workplace in which seven men were shot to death by a disturbed fellow employee—in Honolulu. In 2003 the Honolulu Police Department and the prosecuting attorney publicly identified the illegal use of crystal methamphetamine, "ice," as a major factor in crimes occurring in Honolulu.

Other common statements heard about town are, "You can't do anything about the crime problem," or "HPD and the prosecutors and the courts need to get tough on crime." We should add the following statement to these: "We need to keep ourselves from becoming victims." Can we do it? Yes, we definitely can! Prevention is the key.

We can do things to prevent ourselves and our homes from becoming easy prey for criminals. We can understand techniques and behaviors that will make it difficult for criminals to choose us as their targets. We can teach our children to be observant and aware of activities that can place them in dangerous or risky situations.

Two basic concepts underlie the principle of prevention: *kīnā'ole* and Excellence of Habit. We talked about *kīnā'ole* in the introduction. Briefly, it is the old Hawaiian concept of doing the right thing the first time.

Excellence of Habit is best described in a statement made more than 2,300 years ago by Aristotle, the Greek philosopher and logical thinker. He said, "We are what we repeatedly do. Excellence, then, is not an act, but a habit."

Excellence is a characteristic of habitual quality. The things we need to do to prevent crime and protect ourselves *must be acts of habit.* They must be acts in which we do the right thing—*the first time.*

Prevention, then, is the key to protecting ourselves in this dangerous world.

14
Your Home Is Your Castle

If you lived in England in the eighteenth century, the common belief was that your home was a very special place. Around the time of the American Revolution, British statesman William Pitt spoke the following words in his speech on a British excise bill:

The poorest man may in his cottage bid defiance to all the forces of the Crown. It may be frail; its roof may shake; the wind may blow through it; the storms may enter, the rain may enter, but the king of England cannot enter; all his forces dare not cross the threshold of the ruined tenement!

But watch out for that burglar! He won't have the same respect for your home as the king of England would have. Burglary is defined as the unlawful entry into your home by someone who has the intent to commit a crime therein.

We've all heard yet another old saying: "If they really want to get in, there's nothing you can do to keep them out." This is not true. There are many things you can do to protect your home. Let's start by looking at your home from the street—just as a burglar would.

What Does Your Yard Look Like?

A home that's inviting to a burglar is one where the yard will conceal his activities. Big, tall fences and walls not only keep out nosy neighbor's eyes but also the searching eyes of passing police officers. And they tend to hide any crook lurking behind them. Beautiful, full hedges add a lush environment to our Hawai'i homes. They also conceal. Talk to your local gardener to find low-growing plants that will not hide a crook standing at your windows. Besides, thick, bushy plants covering your windows tend to become a place for insects to congregate.

If you do have a fence, secure it with a padlock. It's the best type of lock for your fence or gate, and many types of padlocks can be purchased that can be keyed to your house key. It's one less key to carry. More important, if you're like me, you won't remember what the key was for anyway. Why make it easy for crooks to simply walk into your yard? Make them climb the fence.

Dogs, Alarms, and Other Noisemakers

Do you have a sign on your fence warning people to beware of your dog—but you don't own a dog? Or is there a sticker on your window alerting all crooks to the fact that you have an alarm system, but all you really have is the sticker? No one can tell you whether that's a good deterrent or not. On the one hand, a meek crook will see the warning signs and move on. A more daring crook will want to see that dog—or at least hear it bark. It's your call. It can't hurt.

One of my students gave me a beware-of-dog sign that had a picture of a malnourished Chihuahua saying, "I can make it to the fence in 2.8 seconds. Can you?" This is cute, but Chihuahuas are just not menacing enough. You need a sign saying, "I own a Rottweiler. Come on in."

If you do own a dog, however, remember it can be a deterrent. It can also be a liability when *tūtū* and niece come selling chicken at your door. Also remember that dog owners who keep vicious animals can be prosecuted if a person is attacked by their dog. And if you purchase an alarm system, you have a series of do's and don'ts that you need to pay attention to.

Alarm Do's
- Make sure you purchase your alarm from a reputable company. The last thing you need is to be ripped off by a *security* company.

- Choose between a system that simply sounds an audible alarm alerting your neighbors and one that includes having the service provider notify the police for you. Remember that here in Honolulu, you can be fined if the police respond to false alarms.
- If you alarm, go all the way. Alarming doors but not windows is a waste of money. Most burglars enter through windows.
- While you're at it, most alarm companies will include in your protection system a fire alarm connected to smoke alarms and hooked up to your siren for a reasonable fee.
- Have your system hardwired but with a battery backup. You don't want to lose alarm service each time Hawaiian Electric Company has a power outage.
- Keep your security code secret within your immediate family. Don't we just love to talk and share things in Hawai'i? Don't give out your alarm code.
- Let your neighbors know you have an alarm and what it sounds like. Can you hear the conversation? "Honey, what's that sound?" "Go back to sleep! It's just some kid's cheap car alarm going off again. It'll go off in a few minutes."

Alarm Don'ts
- Don't spend money for an alarm system and then not use it.
- Don't make your code too difficult, but change it from the default one set by the alarm installer. This is not to say that the alarm installer is a burglar, but stranger things have happened, right? Or maybe the alarm guy, who is also a part-time burglar, will always program the same number at all of his installations—and then revisit them later because many homeowners fail to change the default code.
- Remember your code. Don't let the alarm go off while you try to figure it out. "Now, was it grandpa's birthday, or the day your father and I got divorced?"
- Remember, too, that the police will fine you for false alarms if they are called to your alarm.

• Don't be irresponsible with your system. An alarm screaming "wolf" will cause your neighbors to no longer pay attention.

If you opt for an alarm system, you may be given a choice between a horn-sounding alarm or a siren. Choose the siren. They're usually louder and have the effect of making sure someone *will* look to find that alarm. Also, the more annoying the alarm, the faster someone will call the police to shut it off.

Windows and Death Traps

When a burglar looks at your windows, does he smile and mouth the word "louver"? Louvered windows are a burglar's best friend. And in Hawai'i, it seems that some architects and contractors take an oath at architect and contractor school to always use louvers. It may be that they're related to Light-Fingered Louie, the Louver Man.

There's a rumor going around that louvers are perfect for Hawai'i's weather. Actually, they're perfect for Hawai'i's burglars. Louvered windows are easier to get into than the crank-style windows you see in some homes today. Some people say that simple sliding windows are easier to break into than louvered windows. Perhaps, but sliding windows can be secured even when open a few inches. Leave a louvered window open and a good burglar can have all of your louvers off in under a minute and in a neat pile right behind the bushy hedge hiding him from the street. And he doesn't mind the bugs crawling all over the window because of that bushy hedge.

While crank-style windows provide a greater measure of security for your home, they're not foolproof either. A skinny burglar can slip in through a wide-open crank-style window. When you're away from home and you want to leave those crank-style windows open, make sure they are open no more than four inches. Force that crook to be anorexic.

If you have louvered windows and haven't yet received that million-dollar check from Ed McMahon so you can have them replaced, there is something you can do. Most hardware stores will sell you a protection package for louvers. It consists of epoxy glue. Yup, you glue those louvers right onto their metal frames. It's not foolproof, but remember, you're trying to prevent a break-in by slowing that burglar down or by causing him to make noise. He may think twice about making lots of noise by breaking your glass louvers.

When my family and I went to a Christmas party deep in Moanalua Valley last year, I noticed that a house near the one we were visiting had large yet decorative wrought-iron bars across all of its windows. The scary thing was that they looked homemade.

Putting bars across your windows will keep out burglars. But they will also keep you locked inside while your house burns down. Unless you get a professional system that has an interior release handle on the inside of each barred window, you can make your home so tightly secured that it becomes a death trap in the event of a fire. Never lock yourself inside with homemade bars without interior release devices—unless, of course, you also plan on wearing horizontal striped clothing and tattooing your identification number on your left bicep. Matching orange outfits also go well with bars.

Outdoor Lighting

Got lights? If not, go get them. Lighting is an easy and fairly inexpensive way to protect your yard and house perimeter. Porch and garage lights along with flood lighting at the corners of your house can make it difficult for a burglar to hide at night. You can also hook lighting systems up to photosensitive motion detectors. I had one once that worked so well that every leaf blowing by set the darn thing off, firing six hundred watts into my neighbor's bedroom window—but only after two in the morning, when, as we all know, leaves fall from trees, blown by the strong wind that howls through the night. It's something to do with their union contract.

Lighting systems don't have to be sterile, gray metal junction boxes that have the look of a commercial warehouse written all over them. There are many shops in Honolulu where you can find decorative lighting that will add beauty to your yard and protect at the same time.

Doors and Locks

As the potential burglar moves through your yard closer to your house, he may focus on your door. What he needs to see is a deadbolt lock. Forget the chain that hooks your door to the jamb. It's a waste of time. A well-placed kick will pop that chain bolt right off. It also goes without saying—one would think—that your exterior doors should all be solid; none of those hollow, paper-thin plywood panels.

Sliding glass doors are popular in Honolulu and make for nice big exits through which burglars can remove even your king-size bed. Keep these sliding doors secure by installing antisliding bars in the lower track. You also need to install simple large-headed screws in the upper track above the door frame to prevent the sliding door from being lifted up and out of its frame. These devices can be purchased as sliding glass door protective packages from most hardware stores.

Control Your Keys

Have you ever seen those ads for a decorative plastic rock that you can keep in the garden to hide your house keys? Need I say more? This practice is absolutely foolish. No, let me use plainer language: It's damn stupid! Experienced crooks know all the common places people hide their keys. Never give a spare key to the cleaning lady if you don't know her very well—unless of course you're willing to bet your valuables that someone she knows but who is unknown to you won't be *borrowing* it to come visit you when you're not around.

If you lose a key, it's more expensive, but much safer, to have a locksmith rekey your locks rather than simply make duplicates. Most of us don't want to spend time and money to rekey our locks—so take a different route. Force yourself to be careful with your keys, and pass this concern along to your children.

A Carport or a Garage? How about a Porte Cochère?

So what do you have? A carport is an open parking space with a roof. It can be attached or detached from your house. A garage is an enclosed carport usually attached to your house. "Porte cochère" is French. See, now you speak French. So go to that French restaurant you've been afraid to visit, and when the maitre d' says something in French, put on that big smile and say "Porte cochère!" And order the *coq au vin*—it tastes like chicken. Actually, a porte cochère is a canopy extending from a building to shelter people getting in and out of vehicles. Not too many people have porte cochères—French guys, mainly.

But if you own a carport, you're probably like a whole lot of other people who leave lots of tools and other valuable yard implements right out in the open. Tools in the open become tools available for any burglar to use against your secure home. Lock them up in a shed or cabinet.

People who own enclosed garages sometimes have even more dangerous tendencies. Some actually leave keys to their house hanging in their garage right next to the back door, figuring that no one can get in if the garage door is down. These people tend to leave many more valuables in the open. If you own a garage with a door, particularly an old one, never assume that a crook can't force that door up. Even if your garage door is down, lock the entry door leading to your house.

House Numbers

Ever watch a police officer driving slowly up your street, turn around, and come back? The odds are good that he's looking for a house he was sent to. It happened to me when I was with the Honolulu Police Department. People have very small numbers on their mailbox and sometimes they're hidden by the pretty flower bush growing around it. Others paint their number on the curb, then cover it with a parked car.

Make sure that you have your house numbers clearly posted on your mailbox, at your curb, or on your house and that they are clearly seen from the street—especially for that police officer with bad eyes. The last thing you want in an emergency, when you need the police or firefighters or paramedics immediately, is to have them wander up and down your street looking for your house.

What about Townhouses and Apartments?

Just about everything mentioned before can be applied to townhouses and apartments. Outdoor shrubbery remains a concern (okay, not so much of a concern if your apartment is on the thirty-fifth floor of your building). But alarms, window treatment, doors, and locks are all areas in high-rises that you need to be careful about—especially the door locks. If you're not the first and original owner, someone else besides you has a key to your front door. Rekey or change the locks. It's a small expense but can save big-time headaches.

Be certain you also lock your windows and sliding glass doors that open out into space—or onto your lanai.

"But why worry about windows on the thirty-fifth floor?" you may ask.

Because some burglars are so stupid, they will actually climb out over your neighbor's railing, hang out into thin air, and try to get onto your lanai and into your apartment. The cops call these guys "cat burglars."

Can We Grease the Rails?

Unlike cats, cat burglars tend to fall occasionally. And from the thirty-fifth floor, it won't matter if they land on their feet. Oh, and if you're thinking that you'll just help him out with his sky-diving practice by greasing your railings—don't.

Your intent by greasing the railing is to make him fall. And *you know* that falling from that height will cause his death. Then *you'll* be the one sitting behind bars—for murder or manslaughter. Lock your windows and doors instead. Let the guy fall on his own, if he's stupid enough to think he's a fly. Orange is not a nice color for a shirt. If you don't believe me, go look in your closet and see if you can find that nice, bright orange shirt.

Excellence-of-Habit Recommendations

- Keep tall bushy hedges and plants from blocking the street view to your windows.
- Lock your fence gates.
- While dogs can be a deterrent, be a responsible owner and ensure that no passerby can be attacked by your animal.
- Be a responsible house alarm owner. Don't let your alarm become known for crying wolf.
- Remember your alarm code and keep it secret.
- Shut your louvered windows when you leave. Open louvers are much too easy to remove.
- Never install bars over your windows without a readily accessible interior release. They can become death traps in a fire.
- Use outdoor lighting to illuminate the exterior of your home. Lighting up the darkness eliminates the hiding places a crook might use.
- Make sure your exterior doors are solid.
- Use deadbolts on the exterior doors.
- Secure your sliding glass door from being lifted out or forced open.

15
Inside Your Castle

Imagine coming home from work and finding that someone broke into your home. You find that he rifled through your goods, through your drawers of clothes, and through your closets, and he threw things on the floor looking for things he wanted. Then you find that your DVD player is missing—and the envelope of cash you kept hidden behind some folders in the nightstand next to your pillow. And that small jewelry box you kept on your bathroom counter is gone. Also missing are some inexpensive earrings and the priceless, tiny, silver-plated pendant that your child gave to you for Christmas thirty years ago engraved with "I love you, Mommy." You feel sad. You get angry.

Now imagine that the burglar broke in at two o'clock in the morning while you were asleep in your bed. That's pretty spooky, huh? Now, you're scared.

Your efforts to protect your home don't stop with making sure that the exterior of your home is secure. You should look just as closely at the inside of your home—at its security features and at the behavior of the people who live there. Some people believe that if they catch a burglar inside their home, he's only interested in theft and will run away when surprised. This is not always true—just ask Eric Kawamoto.

On June 26, 2003, Eric Kawamoto came home from work at 4:30 P.M., walked into his house, and confronted a seventeen-year-old burglar. The burglar shot him and fled. Kawamoto was taken to The Queen's Medical Center with a bullet in his chest. He nearly died. But he survived his wound, and the youth was eventually captured and charged as an adult with attempted murder. The youth, through his public defender, told the jury that he didn't mean to shoot Mr.

Kawamoto. It was Kawamoto's fault. If Kawamoto hadn't tried to fight him off, if he was allowed to simply leave (with pockets stuffed so full of Kawamoto's jewelry and other goods that his pants were falling down), if they didn't struggle, then the gun would not have gone off—accidentally—two times. The first shot was a dud and the youth had to eject the dud round, chamber a second round, point the gun at Kawamoto's chest, and shoot him.

The jury didn't believe the youth's far-fetched story. He was convicted and sentenced to spend the rest of his life in prison. So is this a happy ending? Ask Eric Kawamoto. Ask his family. Ask his neighbors. Ask anyone who has come home to find their home trashed by a burglar.

There are things you can do that will help protect you while you are at home. Let's take a look at some of them.

Lights

Leave at least one light on, both inside and outside, when you're away from home, especially if you know you will not be back until after dark. This will provide you with illumination when you enter your house. Nighttime burglars don't like lights and may even go to the trouble of turning off the light you left on. There's your clue that something could be—or is—very wrong.

If you find that the inside lights you left on are now off, but the rest of the neighborhood lights are working, don't be ashamed to call the police to enter your home before you do if you think someone has entered your house. That's their job—to protect and serve. And if you get a response from a cop that implies you're wasting his time, tell the chief of police, because he really wants to know about officers who give a bad image to all the rest of the great men and women who serve on the Honolulu Police Department. Ask almost any police officer; he'll agree that he should enter first. If he doesn't, remind him about Eric Kawamoto.

When you go away for an extended period of time, put timers on some of your lights.

"But the cost," you say. "What about the cost?"

Actually, you can buy some very long lasting electric light bulbs for a little more than the regular ones you would buy. Use these for the lights you'll leave on when you're out. Timers may cost a little more, but they can be a deterrent. When a burglar who is casing your house sees a light go on, he may just leave. And a timer will help reduce the electricity expense by turning on the light only when you want it to.

Panic Room: A Room of Safety

Have you seen the movie *Panic Room?* It's about a woman and her daughter at home who retreat to their panic room when people enter their home and threaten them. Did you realize that you already have a room that you can call your panic room? It's your master bedroom. With a few inexpensive modifications, you can turn your master bedroom into a room that is a safe haven in your home.

First, ensure that the door to your master bedroom is solid; none of those hollow plywood doors for you. Be sure you have a high-quality lock or install one now. If you can find some that have a combo deadbolt, even better. On the inside, add one more feature to help secure the door firmly: metal rod braces. These have U-shaped prongs at one end and rubber feet at the other and when placed up against the doorknob, they help to prevent the door from being kicked in.

If your master bedroom does not have a telephone, consider having one installed. Get a cordless phone. It will give you freedom of movement while you call for help. In addition, many people today have cell phones. If yours is not on your waist, make its home away from your body your master bedroom. Keep its charger in your room—it will help remind you to keep the cell phone there.

Stock your master bedroom with at least one flashlight, a spare set of batteries, and a portable fire extinguisher. If your master bedroom is on the second floor, you may wish to purchase a roll-out ladder that you can hook onto your window. These ladders are designed to help you escape from a fire, but they certainly can be used to escape from intruders intent on harming you.

If you choose a panic room concept and you're single, close and lock your door when you go to sleep at night—every night. If children or other family members live with you, teach them to escape to your panic room at the first indication of trouble or home invaders, except when there is a fire. In a fire, their first action should be to get out of the burning building.

Ding-Dong: Avon Calling

Have you ever had a stranger show up at your door, in spite of your signs that tell them not to solicit at your residence or to watch out for your killer dog? It's going to happen. A potential problem for us in Hawai'i is that our aloha culture bids us to open the door to these strangers—even the people who sell religion door-to-door—smile, and politely hear what they have to say. We've been brought up that way—to be polite, to be friendly, to be welcoming. So we need to temper this welcoming aloha spirit with a sense of caution. You can do this by checking on the person *before* you open the door.

Peepholes are a precautionary step to simply opening your door wide to a stranger. They are not expensive, nor are they difficult to install. You can do it yourself or have a handyman do it. Peepholes allow you to see who is waiting at your door before exposing yourself to potential risk. Another form of observation can be glass panels in your solid front entry door. But perhaps the most common in Hawai'i is the screen door.

You hear people say, "Years ago, we never locked our house." This is usually followed immediately by its counterpart, "Locking the doors is an absolute must nowadays." This also applies to the screen door. Get and use a screen door that is solidly made and has a quality lock—not the $19.95 model that bends with a strong Kona wind. Preferably, get a screen door with a metal mesh that cannot be cut with a razor blade. It's called a security door. Some models have locks that require a key. They're decoratively made so they don't look like jail bars, but they allow you to keep your solid front entry door open and get the cool breeze Hawai'i is known for while providing you with sufficient security to keep an unwanted stranger from pushing his way into your house.

Screen door or not, it's not a good practice to invite a stranger who appears at your door into your home. A discussion on why they're there can be held through your locked screen door or a solid front entry door that is open a few inches but secured by a chain bolt. Remember, some ingenious burglars want to get inside to "case out" your home. What do you have that they might want to come back and steal? How will they get in? Do you have security measures? Hey, keep 'em guessing.

And if you have children, teach them that they are not to open the door when the doorbell rings. That's your job. If a little kid opens the door to a home invader, all of a sudden that invader has a hostage and you will find yourself doing anything he wants. So teach your children to let the adults open the door.

Another Hawai'i practice is entering our homes via the garage or carport door. That's fine for family but not for strangers. Invite someone at your rear or garage door to go to your front door. If you have an enclosed garage, keep the garage door closed. Strangers should not be allowed into areas of your home—even the outside areas that were not intended to be specifically shared with the general public. In other words, limit access by strangers to your home to the front door.

Okay, you're home alone and someone starts banging on your door shouting for help or tells you that they have had an emergency and need to use the telephone immediately. What do you do? Be a good Samaritan and call for them. It's easy to call 911 and ask for a police officer. And tell them it's an emergency. That's what the stranger is telling you, right? In this manner, you get to help the person in need, but you also present to them the fact that you've called for the police.

Never admit to someone at your door that you are home alone.

Fake it. As you approach the door, call out loudly, "I'll get it honey, you can keep cleaning your gun," or "I'll get the door, George—hang onto the pit bull." People who don't know tend to believe you. On Halloween a few years ago, a group of rowdy teenagers came to my door and some of them walked to the gate at the side of my house, opened it, and started to walk toward my backyard. I called out loudly, "Watch out for the dog! He bites. And make sure you close the gate; he'll chase you." It took only a few seconds and the group that was trick-or-treating—or rather trick-and-retreating—called out for some candy from the safety of the sidewalk. And teach your kids to never, ever tell a stranger outside your front door, "My mommy and daddy are not home."

Remember, every time you open your door to a stranger standing on your porch, you could be placing yourself at some risk. So never be embarrassed to speak to a stranger from behind a closed door or through a small opening. But don't take this too far and *not* answer the door when a stranger calls. He may actually be a burglar trying to see if someone is at home. Failing to answer the door may be an invitation to this burglar to break into your house.

Apartment Complexes

If you live in a high-rise apartment building and access into the building is via an intercom system, never open the building's secure entry to someone you don't know or someone you're not expecting. It is wiser to refer these people to the building's manager. If the stranger objects to your notifying management, call the police and notify them of a suspicious person trying to get into your apartment building. Once you allow a stranger into a locked apartment complex, you have placed all residents at risk.

Remember that some criminals search mailboxes for the names of women. A woman's name usually signifies that a woman is living alone. She can become a criminal's target and potentially his victim. If you're a woman living alone in an apartment complex, and your name must be on your mailbox, you should always keep that name neutral or looking as if a family lives there. If your name is Alicia Wong, just use Wong or A. K. Wong. It's better to use more than one initial because some crooks figure one initial to be a woman. Preferably, use The Wong Family or The Wongs. It gives the impression that other people live in that apartment.

Help! There's Someone in My House

If someone breaks into your home while you are there and you have the opportunity to avoid a confrontation, avoid coming face-to-face with the burglar. Run out of your house if you can. If you cannot, flee to your safe room, your panic room. Lock your door immediately. Call the police immediately. Tell the operator who answers the call that you have an emergency. You'll be switched to a police dispatcher as soon as possible. Be absolutely certain to tell the police dispatcher that the crime is occurring now and that you are at risk. Give the police dispatcher as much information as possible. Stay on the phone with the dispatcher and wait for the police to arrive. Be alert and prepared to react if confronted or accosted.

Most burglars will run when confronted, but you can't count on that. If confronted, try to remain calm. Be cooperative. Your possessions are not worth losing your life over. If you must defend yourself, *defend your life,* not your property.

After you have called the police, shout out loudly to the intruder, "I have called the police! I have called the police! The police are on the way. " If they hear you, hopefully they will run away as fast as their crooked little legs will carry them. The police will try to get to your home as quickly as possible.

Excellence-of-Habit Recommendations
- Leave at least one light on, inside and outside your home, when you expect to return after dark.
- Use a timer to turn on and off your lights when you're away from home for an extended period of time.
- Turn your master bedroom into a safe haven—a panic room.

- Screen strangers who come to your door. Use peepholes.
- If someone comes to your door asking for help, offer to make the call for them.
- Never admit to a stranger that you're home alone.
- Ensure that your screen door is of high quality with a strong lock to prevent someone from cutting the screen, reaching in, and unlocking the door.
- If you live in an apartment building, never let a stranger into the building complex.
- If you are a woman, never put your full name on your mailbox.
- If an intruder enters your home while you are inside, run away if you can; otherwise, retreat to your panic room and call 911.
- If confronted by an intruder, try to remain calm and cooperate. Your property is never worth your life.
- If you must defend yourself, defend your life, never your property.

16
Self-Awareness and Street Smarts

When you read through these pages, you may say to yourself, "My, what a horrible, awful world we live in!"

Of course, we know it's not such a terrible world. Think of the words to the song "It's a Wonderful World," written in 1967 by George Weiss and Bob Thiele expressly for Louis Armstrong, who made it famous. Whenever I hear that song, about the beauties of nature, about friends and family, it helps me shake myself free of the paranoia I developed as a police officer and come to the realization that 99 percent of the people I will come across are good people.

But I can never forget that 1 percent may be plotting to do me— or you—harm. So you and I should always go though life *aware* of our surroundings and *aware* of the situations we are in to prevent harm from coming to us.

Let's look at some situations in which we can adapt our behavior to prevent harm from coming to us while maintaining Louis Armstrong's belief about our wonderful world.

Walking and Walking and Walking
Confidence

When you walk, are you confident of yourself? Does your manner say to everyone, "I know who I am, I know where I'm going, and I'm not afraid"? Or when people look at you do they see someone looking down at the pavement, looking nervously about, and acting like they wished they were already home or that the next person is going to punch their lights out?

Timid, helpless-looking people are crook magnets. If you present this image, you're the person the crook will approach and demand your wallet. Crooks, while generally stupid people, know enough not to pick on the person likely to give them trouble. They would much rather choose someone who looks like they have no self-confidence.

Let's look at why you should be confident. By knowing that the majority of people are good, you now need to turn your attention to the situations in which you put yourself. Most of your daily life will be in situations in which you can feel confident and safe. But at the same time, you realize that one percent of dangerous people may enter your safe world. So to develop confidence, you must ensure that you are able to recognize and be aware of those situations and react accordingly. It is in the way you react that you build confidence.

Contact with a Stranger on the Street

Face it. When you walk around town, the shopping mall, or inside a store, you're going to run into strangers. And some of them will look to you like they just escaped the *maison de lune*. See, I told you I understood French.

It is perfectly all right to look at people, even with a momentary direct look in their eyes. Good manners call for a brief nod—maybe even a slight smile to accompany the eye contact. The person who intends no harm will generally smile and nod back. While walking about, though, you will find that all people will require that their personal space be acknowledged—yourself included.

Personal Space

When someone gets too close to you, you involuntarily move to get back your personal space. When that person who falls into the 1 percent makes an effort to get too close to you, you have the right to defend your space. Take a deliberate step away. If he continues, put your hand out in front of you with your palm up. Say "Excuse me" and move another step away—and now pay particular attention to that person. You're setting your boundary. It's also a sign of confidence and that you're paying particular attention. You're no longer an easy target for a crook.

Sidewalks and "God, I'm Being Followed!"

Walk in the middle of the sidewalk. It keeps you away from the street and gives you a little more room and a brief moment to see people approaching you from the side.

Never carry your purse or bag on the street side of you. Some crooks try to make a living by driving slowly in a car close to the sidewalk and having an associate crook reach out from the car to grab bags. We had a case in which a woman's handbag was hanging from her shoulder. A crook in the passenger seat of a car reached out to grab her bag. He did. But it caught on her arm and pulled her into the street and under the rear tires of the suspect's vehicle. She was run over and taken to The Queen's Medical Center in critical condition.

Walk toward traffic if you can. You can see the vehicles approaching. If you're being followed by a car, cross the street.

If you're being followed on foot, change direction. If the crook changes direction with you, cross the street. If he follows, go immediately into the nearest open store where other people are or go to any nearby location where you can be with other people. If you have a cell phone, call and tell someone where you are. Call the police. If you are confronted or attacked, scream for help at the top of your lungs. Some people recommend shouting "Fire!" instead of shouting "Help!" Shout something—"Fire!" or "Help!" or "Rape!"—anything loud enough to get the attention of other people and to make the crook realize that other people are looking at him.

Accepting a Ride

This is a simple paragraph to write. Never accept a ride from a person you don't know. And never accept a ride from a person you may have met briefly unless you're sure you trust him with your life, even when it's raining or you have car trouble. It doesn't get any simpler than that.

When you accept a ride, you place yourself at the mercy of the person picking you up. Ted Bundy murdered more than twenty women who accepted his offer of rides. Sometimes he made sure they had car trouble to get them to accept a ride.

It's very simple: Never accept a ride from a person you don't know. And never accept a ride from a person you have known only briefly unless you trust that person with your life.

Elevators

When you enter elevators, stand near the control panel and the door. If trouble occurs, sweep your hand and fingers down the control panel. Light up as many of the floors as you can. And press the elevator alarm. The alarm will then scream out. Then you scream and keep screaming. Crooks don't like drawing attention to themselves. Your screaming and the elevator alarm going off when the door next opens will attract attention.

When the door opens, force yourself out. If struggling with the crook, make sure you at the very least block the door open. The elevator won't move if the door is blocked open.

Your struggle and screams may be enough to cause the crook to run away when the elevator comes to a stop.

A Final Word

Anyone can suggest to you what to do in the event you are attacked. It's all just words—well-meaning as they may be. The reality is that when you're attacked, fear fills your body. Adrenaline fills your body. A desperate desire to flee fills your body. The world seems to move in slow motion. You may or may not feel pain. And all those well-meaning words are nowhere to be found. Helplessness sets in. What can you do?

You can practice. Occasionally tell yourself, okay, a man has grabbed me as I walk along and is trying to pull me into his car. What do I do? Now run through your mind a simple response: I will scream, fight, kick, punch, bite, claw, and do anything—anything— to protect my life.

Remember that.

Excellence-of-Habit Recommendations

- Believe that the vast majority of people you have met and who you will ever meet are good. But be aware of your surroundings and situations to protect yourself from those bad guys who make up the 1 percent who could do you harm.
- Remember that a timid-looking person is an easier target for a crook.
- Confidence can be yours as long as you believe in yourself and your ability to recognize dangerous situations.
- Don't cower around a stranger. Recognize his personal space and act like you know you have a right to your personal space.
- Protect your personal space when someone intrudes.
- Walk in the middle of the sidewalk.
- Walk facing traffic.
- If followed, change direction. If you're still uneasy, go where other people are.
- In elevators, stand near the door and the control panel.
- If attacked in an elevator, light up all the floor buttons and scream. Block the door with your body as you make an attempt to escape, screaming all the time.
- Scream anything. Scream loud. Scream a lot. Crooks don't like screams.
- Never accept a ride from a person you don't know. And never accept a ride from a person you don't know well enough to trust with your life—literally.

17
The Little Old Lady from Pasadena

Unlike the little old lady from Pasadena, you should not be speeding. And I don't care if you accuse me of using clichés. Speed kills. We see the headlines so very often. "Three killed in crash on freeway: Police say speeding involved."

And you hear comments such as, "It's okay if they only kill themselves." Unfortunately, innocent people die because of some speeding fool.

Racing

What's in vogue today for some teenagers and young adults?

- A small foreign car.
- A suspension system modified so that it sits just a few inches off the ground. Why? For a lower center of gravity. Why? So it can go faster.
- A modified fuel injection system. Why? So it can go faster.
- A modified exhaust system (with a really big tail pipe). Why? So it can go faster.

You've seen them: small cars a few inches off the road that sound like a souped-up lawnmower. And when you see them, they're always speeding. I've had the very unfortunate experience of hearing and seeing two of these death machines speed past my house. Seconds later, one crossed the center line and crashed into an oncoming car. Two people were dead in a tangled mess of several thousands of pounds of metal—one of them who had been innocently driving home. The other was his killer.

Recently, four men were killed on the freeway. Two of these death machines were racing. They plowed into the rear of a truck preparing the zipper lane for morning traffic on the freeway. One of the men who died was an innocent person trapped in the truck when the truck's fuel tank exploded. He died in the flames because the impact knocked him out and he was pinned inside the cab of the truck. His coworker tried to free him from the cab and could have easily died alongside him.

The people who recklessly speed don't care. With so many deaths over the years because of racing, you would think they would learn. They haven't.

Who is "they?" Usually they are young people, both males and females who have a false belief that speeding is their "culture."

How do they get these cars? In too many sad cases, their parents buy the cars for them. Even more sadly, those parents say later, "I couldn't control him."

What can you do to protect yourself from this danger?
- Be aware of your surroundings when you drive.
- Don't just look straight ahead. Look in your rearview mirror.
- When people are speeding or racing behind you, let them pass. If you can, change lanes and get out of their way.

Perhaps more important, complain to the police. Complain to your state representative, and your senator, and your council member. Be a thorn in their sides, because they haven't taken the action necessary to stop this terror on our roadways.

Work with your neighbors, your church, or your club to find others who want to protect the community. Then make yourself heard.

Road Rage

Inevitably, with so much tension in drivers, someone is going to say or do something stupid to another person while driving. If this happens to you, let the fool drive by. Don't challenge him. Keep yourself safe.

If the fool begins to follow you, drive to the nearest police station. Call the police while you drive there. Maintain a safe speed and do nothing to provoke the fool who is harassing you—except of course to get his license number to give to the police.

The Drunk Driver

Far too many people drive drunk. It's part of our American vehicle culture, didn't you know? It's "all right" to drink. It's even okay to drink until you're falling-down drunk. But wait. I mean, even the booze commercials tell you to have a designated driver. That means I can get as drunk as I like as long as someone else drives. Ever try to tell a falling-down drunk that he can't drive? Every one of them is absolutely certain he is perfectly capable of driving. Ask former police officer Clyde Arakawa. During Arakawa's trial for causing the death of a young woman after having consumed enough booze to put a horse to sleep and having driven his car while drunk, speeding, and running a red light, his attorney had the audacity to tell the court that Arakawa was not drunk owing to the fact that his liver processed booze better than the rest of us because he drank so much so frequently.

Wow! I never heard that one before.

So what can you do to protect yourself from drunk drivers? It's pretty much the same as for the speeding racers: Pay attention. Be aware of the drunk driver and get out of his way. Look for the following:

- Weaving, either from lane to lane or weaving within the borders of a single lane.
- Speeding up and slowing down.
- Stopping well beyond the stop line at intersections.
- A driver who looks sleepy or is slouched in the driver's seat.

If you see someone like him, call the police. They may get lucky and find him on the roadway before he kills someone. Here's what we can do as a community:

- Complain to the police.
- Complain to your state representative, your senator, and your council member.

• Find others who will work to stop this terror on our roadways.

So far, we've talked about a few things that other people do. Now let's look at ourselves.

Seat Belts

Use them—all the time. Make your children use them. Make your young ones use safety seats for kids. Make sure you install them properly, with the right car seat for the right age and weight. And use booster seats for children until they are tall enough to have seat belts fit them properly. Have children sit in the backseat—never in the front seat of a car with an air bag. Air bags can kill children and even small adults.

Don't let anyone take his seat belt off as you near your destination. This is for the simple reason that you're not there yet. Use your own seat belt; otherwise you're sending the wrong message. Seat belts save lives. Use them—period.

Parking

Before you park your vehicle in a parking garage, leave your doors locked until you look around to see if anyone is lurking nearby. If you see a person or a situation that makes you feel unsafe, go find another stall nearer the attendant's booth. Or look for another parking location altogether. Never feel forced into that one parking spot.

Never park and get out of your car if you feel you are being followed. And never drive home if you feel you're being followed. Go to a busy gas station. Go to the nearest police station and report the license number and make of the car following you.

When you are walking back toward your car and you have a remote device to unlock your door, don't unlock your door while you are too far away from your vehicle. If someone is waiting at your vehicle, don't approach it if you are alone. Walk away to where other people are and call the police.

Always look inside your car before getting in. Someone may have broken in and be hiding, waiting for you to get in.

Help! My Car Broke Down Again

When you have car trouble, make sure you pull completely off the roadway, if possible, to remove yourself and your car from the traffic. If you can still drive the vehicle, drive to the nearest service station.

It's a good idea to carry several flares in your trunk and put on your flashing emergency signals. If someone stops ask them to call the police for you, if you haven't done so already. Never accept a ride from strangers.

Excellence-of-Habit Recommendations

- Beware of people who are racing. Get out of their way immediately if you can do so safely.
- Watch for drunk drivers. Know the symptoms that will alert you that a driver is drunk: weaving, speeding up, and slowing down.
- Don't argue with a driver displaying road rage.
- Don't gesture at other drivers.
- Use your seat belts.
- Make your children use their safety seats, booster seats, and seat belts.
- Be aware and alert when parking your vehicle.
- Never approach your car if someone is lurking near it.
- If your vehicle breaks down, call the police for help. Wait inside the car.
- When approaching your car with kids, get the kids, then yourself inside, and lock your doors. After this, you can concentrate on getting the kids into their safety seats, booster seats, and seat belts from inside the locked car.
- If you drive alone, drive with doors locked and windows shut. If you don't have air conditioning, leave the windows open only a few inches when you must stop for traffic lights or stop signs.
- Before getting into your car, look to see if someone is hiding inside.

- Be aware of people and cars around you at stop signs and red lights.
- If you are being followed, head for a police station.
- If someone tries to pull you into a car, resist any way you can. Do anything you need to do to save your life, then run away. Nothing good comes from being abducted.
- If someone tries to forcibly enter your car, blow your horn and drive off. Never worry about him falling down.
- Call the police and report any suspicious instance or any event in which someone is trying to harm you or your passengers.

18
Workplace Safety

Every so often you hear about an employee of some company killing fellow employees. The slang term for it is "going postal." Some years back, the post office campaigned to eliminate or discourage the term. Workplace violence, they said, happens everywhere, not only at the post office. And they're right. The Xerox Corporation had an extremely deadly occurrence of workplace violence in which seven men were murdered by Byran Uyesugi on November 2, 1999. And those families will never forget. One way to show respect to them is to do what you can in the future to protect yourself and others.

"But there's nothing you can do when somebody goes postal," people say.

This is not so. There's a lot people can do. There's a lot people should know about workplace violence. First of all, what is violence?

A common definition includes much more than bringing a rifle to work and shooting people. Violence is the abuse or unjust exercise of power. It's an outrage or a wrong against an employee. It's physical assault causing harm to another. And it includes the "attempt" to do any of these things. It can be committed by any employee of an organization, from the lowest level to the chief executive officer.

With this definition, violence can come in many forms. It includes verbal abuse, harassment, threats, pushing, shoving, and sexual assault, to identify a few types. Violence can happen anywhere in an organization, from the loading dock to the administrative offices, elevators, parking lots, and stairways. Understand, though, that the type of workplace violence exhibited by the murderous rage of Byran Uyesugi is rare. Usually workplace violence consists, for example, of an argument between coworkers. And remember, it can happen again. In the Xerox case, some of those men who died had earlier reported warning signs.

The cost of workplace violence is high. The obvious effects are injuries, financial loss, anger, frustration, and confusion. One more subtle cost is the fear of victimization. We all fear becoming a victim of crime, but when crime happens near us, our fear of becoming a victim increases. This can have a detrimental effect on our jobs and family life. We become paranoid and nervous, always looking over our shoulder for that criminal who may be lurking and waiting to do us harm. Police officers often suffer from these feelings after seeing many crimes and victims in their lives.

Warning Signs

We sometimes forget that there are warning signs associated with workplace violence—signs given to us by the employee who may potentially become violent. We may see one or all of the following:

- Screaming at others
- Swearing
- Challenging authority
- Threatening people
- Using violent gestures
- Drinking alcohol or using drugs
- Blaming others for mistakes
- Using "I'll get even" statements

You may hear that the employee has marital trouble and his personal life seems to be falling apart. You may see a change of dress, from clean and well kept to sloppy and dirty. He may have a preoccupation with guns.

As an employee, if you observe any of the above warning signs, tell your supervisor. One big problem among people in general is that they usually "don't want to get involved."

You'd better get involved—or you may one day become one of his victims.

"What can we do?" you ask. Read on.

Prevention

Prevention is the key. Be prepared and be aware. Stay alert. Be confident and take charge of your own safety.

The first and foremost thing to do to prevent workplace violence is to treat every person, employee or not, with respect. Trust your gut feelings and watch for the warning signs. If at all possible, be responsible and head off trouble before it turns to violence. One way to do this is to report the warning signs to your supervisor. If he doesn't do anything, go higher. You could be saving your life or others.

When trouble does occur at work, try to stay calm. Yes, we know that's easier said than done. But keeping your head when things get out of hand can save your life. The first thing to do is to escape the building. The only way you can do this as fast as possible and as easily as possible is to know your workplace. Identify escape routes from your office and walk them every so often. It's good to know as many ways out of your building as possible for many reasons: Fire is the obvious one.

Safety at Work

Here are some things you can do to be safe at work:

- Know and understand security measures offered by your employer. For example, if your organization is a twenty-four-hour operation but locks its doors at a specific hour, *keep the danged door locked!* It's for your safety, not to be a pain in the butt. So you have to use one security or monitored door if you want to go outside to smoke a cigarette. When you open doors that are supposed to be secured when the building is locked, or when you prop open a door as a shortcut, it becomes an unauthorized entry for all kinds of people who may have all kinds of criminal intentions.

- Never—*never*—give out personal information on employees to callers. Private information must never be given to others without their permission. A young woman who was being abused by her violent husband finally found enough courage to run from him. She found safety in a shelter and eventually was able to get a divorce from him. Just when she felt that her life was becoming normal again, a woman called her employer. The woman said she was from calling from California and was trying to reach the young woman because there was a death in the family. The caller was given the young woman's address. That night, the woman's ex-husband broke into her home and nearly beat her to death. Again, *never* give out personal information on employees to callers, even if it sounds like an innocent request or an emergency. Offer to take a telephone number and try to get in touch with the employee yourself. You would want someone to do the same for you.
- Keep visitors to your organization out of work areas where they do not belong. A visitor is just that, and safety insists that visitors remain in controlled, neutral areas.
- At the end of the workday, walk to your car or parking lot with other employees. There's safety in numbers.
- If you have to work late, let your family know, and check in with someone about your schedule and whereabouts.
- Be assertive about unwanted sexual attention at work. If you are a victim of sexual harassment at work, you can bet your last dollar that the man harassing you is harassing other women as well. By remaining quiet, you empower the sexual harasser to continue his bad behavior. Tell your supervisors immediately. They are obligated to stop the man. If they don't, they are liable for great damages in civil court. Assert yourself and help make our world a fair one for all men and women.
- Never leave your valuables unattended. If you're lucky enough to have a locker, use it and keep it locked. We had a theft in which the victim had money stolen from his locker. When

asked if the locker was locked, he replied, "No, I can't remember the combination, so I keep it open." Tell that to your insurance company. Never tell other employees that you are carrying valuables or large sums of cash. A young woman came back from Las Vegas a winner—a big winner, at least in my eyes. She had $12,000 in cash and flashed it at work, excited about her good fortune. She put the money in her purse, put her purse in her desk, and went to lunch. When she returned, her small fortune was gone and she was brokenhearted that one of her "friends" would steal her money. Use your common sense. Theft is characterized as having desire and opportunity: The crook has the desire and we give the crook the opportunity. Let's make it difficult for crooks to steal.

- If you work in an office, where's your purse when you go to the bathroom? Is it in the bottom drawer on the right? Where's your checkbook—in the center drawer? Remember, some thieves know those hiding places, too.

Excellence-of-Habit Recommendations

- Understand workplace violence and know its warning signs.
- Report all warning signs and/or violence to your employer.
- Report all instances of sexual harassment.
- Know and understand security measures offered by your employer.
- Keep your valuables secured.
- Never give out personal information about an employee to anyone.
- Walk to your car with other workers after work.
- Tell people your schedule and whereabouts when working late.

19
Preventing Sexual Assault

Unfortunately, a common thought about sexual assault among many women is that "it can't happen to me." Sadly, it can. Sexual assault victims have been women and girls of all ages, of all ethnic backgrounds. The rapist does not care whether his victim is attractive or not, whether she is married or not. Even pregnant women have been victims, along with the rich and the poor and everyone in between. Men and boys have also been victims.

Fortunately, understanding what you can do to prevent rape is a big step toward preventing its happening to you.

Understand first that sexual assault and rape are forms of violence. The rapist's intent is to dominate the victim through his forcible sexual assault. Understanding that rape is a crime of violence points to ways to prevent it.

Rape by a Stranger

When a stranger rapes, there is a strong likelihood that he is a criminal looking for a victim of opportunity. So the best defense, as with the prevention of theft, is to remove the opportunity for the rapist to make you his victim.

In earlier chapters, we've discussed the many ways to safeguard your home. Physical security for your home, making your bedroom a safe haven, and being aware of and alert to your surroundings and behavior are some of the important points.

"I have my rights to be who I am and not have to worry about how I behave," you say.

Yes, but there is truth in the statement that putting oneself in dangerous situations raises your risk of becoming a victim. A woman who hitchhikes places herself at a greater risk of becoming a victim than one who does not. Someone who goes to a bar alone and drinks herself stupid is at a greater risk than one who consumes alcohol responsibly. Some behaviors, while protected by the freedoms we have in our country, place people at greater risk than those who approach situations with more caution.

The best defense against rape by a stranger is to have a secure home and to conduct yourself in a responsible manner.

Date Rape

Date rape is also known as acquaintance rape. There's the key word: "acquaintance." An acquaintance is someone you do not know well or someone you recently or briefly met.

Would you give an acquaintance, or someone you recently met, your life savings and say, "Hang on to this for me. I'll be back tomorrow to pick it up"? It's the same when meeting a man and becoming acquainted with him. The common-sense, responsible thing to do is to get to know him over a period of time rather than run off to his "chalet" for a drink, where you might be quite isolated. For all you know, his "chalet" is one room in a boarding house that he has rented for a week.

Again, we come back to responsible behavior. As a society, we meet and enjoy people's company, but the responsible action is to meet them in public places until you are comfortable being alone with them. Don't give out your home address and home telephone number to men you have just met. Don't get in cars alone with strangers. Remember that most date rapes occur at an isolated place, in an apartment, or in a car.

"Okay, I've seen this guy about five times with a group of friends. He seems nice and he asked me out to dinner—just him and me. I accepted."

That's great. He's probably a wonderful person. But if he gets sexually aggressive the first time you're out with him and it's unwanted, it's not the time to be meek and weak. Tell him immediately that his behavior is unwanted and that he must stop. If you want him to stop, don't even hint at weakness on your part. Be firm, use a loud voice, and stop his actions. Set boundaries and let him know you're confident about yourself and what is acceptable and that you will speak up and take action.

Date Rape Drugs

There is one surefire way to prevent someone from sneaking a date rape drug into your drink when you're not looking. Always be looking. Be in control of your glass. It stays in your hand or in your view.

"But I gotta go to the bathroom!"

Finish your drink, then go. If you can't wait, and you have to leave your drink, feed it to the plant or the cat when you return and go get a fresh new one.

"That can get expensive."

Then hang on to your drink.

Taking away the opportunity for a stranger to put a date rape drug in your drink is the prevention here. What does it require?

• Responsible drinking
• Attentiveness and alertness when in the company of strangers
• Control of your drinks and food items

What Can a Woman Do?

One drastic approach is what some moms tell their "marryin' age" daughters: "You don't need a man. What do you need a man for? Get a good job. Make money. Buy a nice house. Travel."

But we humans like companions. So women need to watch for some signs that a man is not being fully honest. Pay attention to some of the following clues:

> • You have no need for any help, but he sure is helpful. Makes you seem downright incapable of doing anything for yourself. "Let me help you get home. Let me help you into the house."
> • "But dear, I *promise* I have nothing but the most respectful intentions." Uh huh.

- "We've just met, but I feel I know so much about you. I would really love to get to know you better."
- "I own a yacht in the Bahamas. I would drive you home in style, but my father has borrowed the Mercedes, and the BMW is in the shop."
- "Let's get away from all this racket and these loud people. We can sit and talk as we listen to the waves. I know a beach where we won't be bothered."
- "You've hurt my feelings. I've been nothing but the perfect gentleman. Won't you let me prove to you I'm sincere?"

Come on, girl. Wake up and recognize the "which line shall I use tonight" syndrome in order to get you alone with him. Dump the loser.

I've Been Raped!

If you have been raped, first of all, your return to safety is important. If you have been attacked in your home, call the police and secure your home as best you can. If you are dropped off on the street, go to where other people may be and ask for help and the police.

The first thing most rape victims want to do is erase that crime from their bodies and minds. But think first. The police will need any kind of evidence they can get to identify your rapist—and much of that evidence may be on your body. So first of all, do *not* bathe. You will be taken to a hospital and treated. A physician who is educated in treating rape victims will recover evidence from you. That evidence will help to apprehend this criminal.

Many rape victims find it excruciatingly difficult to admit they were raped. Seek help, both medical and psychological, but don't hide this crime. There are many support groups to help women recover from rape. And as a former police officer, I ask all rape victims to help us catch the man who hurt you.

I also stress that rape victims seek counseling. This is not a time to tough it out or go it alone. There are many services available to sex assault victims, most of which are confidential.

Excellence-of-Habit Recommendations
- Every woman can become a rape victim.
- Sexual assault is a crime of violence.
- You are at more risk of rape from acquaintances than from a stranger.
- Excessive drinking or taking of drugs impairs your good judgment and places you at a greater risk of becoming a victim of sexual assault.
- It is important to set clear limits with the men you date.
- There is some safety in numbers—never go out alone with a man you don't know or have just met.

20
A Final Word

In the world of law enforcement, we find ourselves trying to learn new and better techniques to locate evidence at crime scenes. Our evidence specialists are becoming better educated and better trained in forensic science and CSI. Currently, the detective in charge of the case is also the person in charge of the CSI. In the early 1990s, I tried to develop a policy in which the person in charge of the CSI would be the evidence specialist, or rather, in my vision, the *forensic evidence specialist*.

My homicide detectives were very good at investigating murders, but I also saw that the evidence specialists who worked with us at crime scenes were often, though quietly, better informed about forensic techniques, procedures, and the science behind them. The detectives would often ask the evidence specialists, "What can you do about this?" or "Is there something you can do about that?"

The detectives knew what they would need to perhaps solve the case, but the evidence specialists knew how, when, and where they might find that evidence. So often I watched evidence specialists, with master's degrees in some scientific field, politely stand there while the well-meaning homicide detective told them to "Pick that up" or "Take a picture of that" or "Don't forget to draw a diagram." I know that the detectives greatly appreciated the specialists, but still, they were the ones in charge.

I did not want the detective removed from the crime scene because he or she needed an intimate knowledge of what happened there. And the detective would still be the one in charge of the overall investigation. What I wanted was to have the expert in CSI become responsible for the crime scene. In my opinion, that responsibility would engender a greater effort, a greater challenge, and perhaps a better discovery of evidence.

Perhaps the biggest problem lies in the statement made by a longtime detective, who could still be shortsighted: "What, a detective answer to a civilian? Never happen!" Human nature and the ongoing battles of turf and ego got in the way.

Well, my idea didn't get too far in present-day law enforcement, and we still have the forensic evidence specialist answering to the detective when it comes to the CSI.

The far more important thing is that when we become victims of crime, in spite of our efforts to protect ourselves, we must remember that there is a small group of experts working in the basement of the Honolulu Police Department who have the knowledge and skill to find the unseen evidence that Locard says *will* be there, process and develop it, testify in court, help convict that criminal who violated our rights, and send him to jail.

And all along they were following the spirit of *kīnā'ole* and Excellence of Habit, perhaps without even realizing it.

"Sometimes it's funny. Sometimes it's frightening. It's never, ever dull."

News@UH

"Dias has a knack for writing in casual vernacular that's the equivalent of being told an entertaining story by a buddy or favorite teacher. And what stories!"

Burl Burlingame,
Honolulu Star-Bulletin

"*Honolulu Cop* is just plain fun to read!"

Bill Taylor,
Hawaii Island Journal

OTHER TITLES IN THIS SERIES

"The husband-and-wife team delivers fresh insights and informed commentary about cases that have been continually but incompletely analyzed and discussed in the community. . . . Unlike other insider authors, Dias checks his respect for his former profession with a clear-eyed appraisal of the difficulties and frustrations that attend the everyday work of homicide investigators."

Michael Tsai,
Honolulu Advertiser

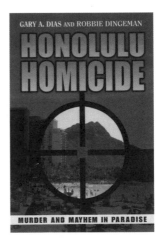